The Hallowing of England

A guide to the saints of Old England and their places of pilgrimage

Fr Andrew Phillips

Anglo-Saxon Books

First Published 1994

Published by
Anglo-Saxon Books
25 Malpas Drive
Pinner
Middlesex
England

Printed by
Antony Rowe Ltd.
Chippenham
Wiltshire
England

British Library Cataloguing-in-Publication Data. A catalogue
record for this book is available from the British Library.

ISBN 1-898281-08-4

Let us now praise famous men,
And our fathers in their generations.
The Lord apportioned to them great glory,
His majesty from the beginning.
There were those who ruled in their kingdoms,
And were men renowned for their power,
Giving counsel by their understanding,
And proclaiming prophecies;
Leaders of the people in their deliberations
And in understanding of learning for the people,
Wise in their words of instruction;
Those who composed musical tunes,
And set forth verses in writing;
Rich men furnished with resources,
Living peaceably in their habitations –
All these were honoured in their generations,
And were the glory of their times.
There are some of them who have left a name.
So that men declare their praise.
And there are some who have no memorial,
Who have perished as though they had not lived;
They have become as though they had not been born,
And so have their children after them.
But these were men of mercy,
Whose righteous deeds have not been forgotten;
Their prosperity will remain with their descendants,
And their inheritance to their children's children.
Their descendants stand by the covenants;
Their children also, for their sake.
Their posterity will continue for ever,
And their glory will not be blotted out.
Their bodies were buried in peace,
And their name lives to all generations.
Peoples will declare their wisdom,
And the congregation proclaims their praise.

Ecclesiasticus 44, 1–15.

Contents

The England to Come

I know Old England shall for ever stand,
Her beauty from beyond shines through this land.
The inward stream of Her forechosen way
Runs in these woods and fields and church towers grey,
And in kind hearts or song by village green,
In homely country lane or meek souls clean,
In farm and hamlet or ancient inn;
Behold Old English life soft flows therein;
Life that springs from spirits by faith made bold,
Who haunt this English land from times of old,
Saints of God fleeting glimpsed by seeing heart.
One I well know he, Godwin, dwells apart;
A thousand years he has prayed by this brook,
His story all untold in learned book,
By eye of man his hallowed life unseen,
But his voice speaks to me in waking dream,
Foreshowing clear that England's history
Shall come aright and tell its mystery,
This thread that unwinds, this tale that unfolds,
The sacred truth that England guards and holds,
The faith and knowledge within Her burning,
Of Christ the Lord at the end returning,
For true and faithful to bring salvation
And fulfil Old England's restoration.

March 1994
Fr. Andrew Phillips

Foreword

The Spiritual Heritage of the Old English Church

Formerly, when men lived in the beauty and bounty of Earth, the reality of Heaven was very near; every brook and grove and hill was holy, and men out of their beauty and bounty built shrines so lovely that the spirits which inhabit Heaven came down and dwelt in them and were companions to men and women, and men listened to divine speech.

John Masefield, Poet Laureate
The Hereford Speech, 23 October 1930

In the year 747 at the Synod of Clovesho under the chairmanship of the saintly Archbishop of Canterbury, Cuthbert, it was recommended that the Feasts of St. Gregory the Great (12th March) and St. Augustine of Canterbury (26th May) be celebrated as national festivals throughout the seven kingdoms of Anglo-Saxon England, as befitted the Apostles of the English. In England the Church was everything. She had given a literature, an art, an architecture, knowledge and learning and she was ready to give national unity. The zeal and faith of the Two Confessors and Apostles of England was making the land into an island of holiness, whose chief export was the saints because that was its natural wealth. England realised itself as the Guardian of Sacred Tradition, the keeper of a sacred trust which it had received directly from the successor of St. Peter. The history of Old England is the history of its Church and the history of its Church is the history of its saints. They were the ones who had one foot in heaven, the other on earth, the ones by whom church life and national life were so closely intertwined, this was a church which was incarnate and yet remained the Church. The disputes of Church and State were for later, much later, and those only the State, by definition, could win; for if the Church were to win them, then it would no longer be the Church, but a Church-State; on the other hand if the State were to win those disputes, the Church would fall totally into erastianism, becoming a State-Church whose very doctrines would be decided by the State and without the spiritual reserves of monasticism to keep its integrity.

In such a brief essay we scarcely have space to record the litany of the names of the English holy ones or to recount their exploits, or the stories of those divine events which saved the Old English Kingdom from spiritual and physical disintegration in the centuries before the Norman Invasion. And yet we cannot but think of certain events and saints who stand out to all. We linger on the intercession of St. Peter who persuaded the disheartened Archbishop Laurence to continue the mission to the English in 616 and again of St. Peter who came down to dwell in spirit in his church at Westminster, raised up by the pious King Sebbe. This was the vision granted by the fisherman to the fisherman. We recall all the Roman followers of Augustine, Sts. Laurence, Mellitus, Peter, Justus and Paulinus, we recall the holy Abbesses of Kent, Ethelburgh, Eanswitha and Mildred. There comes to mind Oswald, who 'toiled for the heavenly kingdom in continual prayer' and became the victor of Heavenfield and now stands in the field of Heaven with his great Cross to the glory of God. There go the holy brothers Chad and Cedd and the faithful monk Owen and the sisters Audrey and Saxburgh with the faithful priest Huna. Here is St. Hilda and the humble herdsman Caedmon the Hymnographer who praised the might of the Creator. We recall the Apostles Aidan, Felix and Birinus, each of a different race, yet united in their task of bringing the English to the Faith. There is the righteous Cuthbert and his soul-friend Herbert of Derwentwater, Cuthbert who 'served the Creator and saw Creation serving him' as he struggled against the jealous demon-hordes off the rugged northern coasts[1]. We remember the great Theodore of Tarsus, the city of Paul, and Abbot Adrian from Africa, shivering in the cold climate, and yet creating a nation out of warring peoples. And Benedict Biscop, that lover of books and icons, stands with the reverend and gentle abbot-saints, Sigfrid, Ceolfrith and Eosterwine. There is Wilfrid who brought stern order to the

---

[1] During the War against Hitler and the Nazis, St. Cuthbert, whose relics are in Durham, protected the city from the Luftwaffe. On the night of the raid, the Saint shrouded the city in dense fog. Similarly, during the Baedeker raid on Canterbury in June 1942, St. Augustine protected Canterbury Cathedral which remained intact, even though one third of the city centre was destroyed.

North and the lowly Alnoth of Stowe and the learned Aldhelm of Malmesbury, each one so very different and yet each one a saint of God. There is the Venerable Bede, the 'candle of the Holy Ghost', whose soul 'longed to see Christ his King in His beauty'. Then Egwin of Worcester who founded the monastery of Evesham on the visions of the Mother of God to the humble shepherd Eves. Guthlac who fought against our ancient foe and who 'spoke with the angels of the heavenly mysteries', whose 'lips gave out a fragrance like unto the scent of the sweetest flowers', whose repose was marked by the appearance of a 'fiery tower reaching from the earth to the height of heaven, turning the light of the sun itself to paleness'. Near his holy sister Pega, stands Bishop John of Beverley, the Wonderworker, and Erkenwald, the patron of London. Nor should we forget those who left these shores to live in holy exile: the holy virgins, Sethrida, Ethelburgh and Erkengota and their companions. Then we see the Greek Pope Zacharias as he blesses Boniface of Crediton, the Patron-Saint of Germany. We turn to Willibrord in Holland and the many companions: Willehad, Lioba, Lull, the holy brothers Ewald and Walburgh the Myrrh-Giver, Sola and Philip of Zell and their helpers in England, Thecla in Wimborne and Cuthbert in Canterbury. Here passes the young shepherd Cuthman who loved the church in Steyning. And that mild and blessed Bishop of Winchester, St. Swithin the English rain-saint, who shone through his miracles. And he of whom it is written; 'the English land is not deprived of the Lord's saints, since in English earth lies . . . the blessed, the wise and honourable, even glorified, amongst men as one of them . . . bountiful to the poor and to widows, ever mindful of the true doctrine' . . . Edmund of East Anglia, King and Martyr who became a true king by choosing, like Christ at Gethsemane, to suffer death at the hands of non-believers rather than defend himself with the sword. We recall those hundreds of martyrs who like him were slain by the Danes. With thankfulness we remember Alfred, honoured amongst the people as a saint until the Reformation. It was he who saved England from the Danes and then converted the dreaded Northmen to the Christian Faith with the help of Sts. Cuthbert and Neot. It was he who restored learning and churchmanship, monasticism and statesmanship, who sent alms to Elias, Patriarch of Jerusalem and further still to India. There goes the holy King of All England, the dream of unity accomplished, Edgar the Peacemaker. Here stand the holy three: St. Dunstan from Glastonbury

11

came forth in the hour of England's need to be the Archpastor of his people, the father of the new spiritual flowering of the nation, together with Oswald the Almsgiver of Worcester and Ethelwald of Winchester, the Father of Monks. And then anew the troubles starting with regicide, the martyrdom of the youthful Edward, King of England, and after the royal martyr, Alphege the Archbishop-Martyr. Or would we think of how Mary the Mother of God saved London in the year 994 at the Feast of Her Nativity,[2] of Wulfstan, Bishop of London, who warned and called to repentance?[3] Or those Englishmen who went out at that time to preach to the still pagan North, of Sigfrid who baptised Anne of Novgorod, of all those who went to Norway, Sweden, Iceland and further still?

In the Old English period we can count over three hundred individual saints known to us, not including the hundreds of nameless martyrs. We have mentioned but few, and then only in passing. And yet not many know their names or their exploits and their lives. They represent a forgotten England, lying on the other side of the Middle Ages – they are our forgotten heritage, an Unknown England because for some nine hundred years spirits have turned elsewhere and this inheritance of the Holy Ghost cast aside by so many, the Living God[4] turned into an idea, a mere concept. The Hallowing of England is the fruit of the Conquest of England by Gregory and Augustine, a half-millennium which hallowed towns and hamlets up and down the land between one Conquest and another. This is our unknown, ignored heritage, our spiritual heritage, our spiritual roots, covered over by centuries of secularism in all its forms. England of the Old English with all its faults was also a land of hallowed bishops and holy kings, of martyr-priests and confessors, of noble princes and princesses, saintly abbesses and humble cowherds, meek hermits and lowly monks, righteous families and silent nuns, faithful queens and gentle abbots, who hallowed it from north to south and east to west. This is the spiritual history and the spiritual

---

[2] This is said to be the origin of the rhyme 'London Bridge is falling down'. 'My fair Lady' refers to the Londoners' prayers to the Mother of God to save them.

[3] St. Alfwold of Sherborne sums up the love of the Old English saints. He reposed in front of the sacred image of St. Swithin, repeating the words of his favourite antiphon to St. Cuthbert.

[4] See the words of the Protomartyr of Britain, St. Alban (Bede Bk. 1, Chapter 7.)

geography of England, created by the end of the first millennium and which we, at the end of the second, have yet to rediscover.

When we examine the Church at the end of the Old English Age, less than five hundred years after the landing of Augustine, after its beginning, we cannot but express wonder at the devotion of the Old English, at the fruit borne of the Garden of Kent. For a population of some 1.5 million, there must have been at least ten thousand churches and chapels, a proportion of 1:150. True, many of them were very small, often founded by guilds of craftsmen, who built these chapels as neighbourhood churches, but even so in modern terms this would equal some four hundred thousand churches. At the Norman Conquest there were thirty-five monasteries and nine convents, numbering some one thousand religious, a proportion of 1:1,500. Moreover, in earlier times before the Viking attacks, we know that even more lived the monastic life. In the time of Bede there were six hundred monks at Wearmouth alone and at Wimborne in the mid-eighth century there were hundreds of nuns. At the Conquest Norwich had a population of some five thousand: so far archaeologists have discovered the sites of forty-nine churches. In Norfolk at about the same time thirteen hundred parishes are recorded. The Domesday Book records for Suffolk a population estimated to be twenty thousand and three hundred and forty-five churches (though many churches were not recorded, the Conqueror did not find them economically interesting).[5] At Bury St. Edmunds there were thirty priests, deacons and clerks for three hundred and forty-two homes, a proportion of 1:11. Moreover as we shall see later, these churches, mostly wooden, contained within them a wealth without comparison in Western Europe with the sole possible exception of Rome.

If we marvel at the piety of the Old English, both in the quantity and the quality of their works of art, we must also look at their devotion to Christ through the saints. If we look at church dedications we find above all a great love for the Mother of God and Virgin Mary and then St. Peter. This

---

[5] Indeed on account of its piety Suffolk became known as 'sælig Suffolk'; in Old and Middle English, 'sælig' means 'blessed'. In modern English this has been corrupted to 'silly Suffolk'. In the same way 'myrige' meaning 'blessed' has been deformed into 'merry' as in 'Merry England', thus changing the original meaning altogether.

was followed by devotion to the Holy Angels (we recall the words of St. Gregory – that the Angles might become Angels), then St. Andrew the Apostle (we recall the monastery on the Coelian Hill in Rome), after St. John the Baptist, St. Nicholas and then the other Holy Apostles. Of that host of home-grown saints the most loved was Cuthbert, that fusion of Saxon and Celtic spirituality. There followed Oswald, Edmund, Swithin, Wilfrid and Chad. The most loved female saints were Hilda, Edith and Audrey. The Apostles of the English were also very popular and dozens and dozens of churches were dedicated to them which, in both cases is remarkable, for St. Gregory never set foot in England and Augustine spent only seven years here.

It is a strange fact that the eleventh century, the last of the Old English Church, was the century when the veneration of St. Augustine flourished the most. Several stories of miracles worked by the saint have come down to us from this time. One miracle occurred in the year 1030. King Canute, like so many English kings and nobles before him, was returning to England from a pilgrimage to Rome. Crossing the Channel, his ship encountered a violent storm and he and the ship were saved only by asking for the prayers of the First Archbishop of the English and Canute's vow to give alms to the shrine of the saint in his monastery. During the abbacy of Abbot Wilfric (1047) at St. Augustine's in Canterbury, a great number of wonders were recorded, wonders which somehow conclude the whole Age, concluding it as it began, with the miracles of a saint of God.

The landing of St. Augustine was the beginning of a peaceful and bloodless invasion by the Word of God of the hearts and minds of all the inhabitants of the English land of good will. It is difficult not to look back at the Old English Church and her saints without love and regret. This was the childhood of England, when our forebears first heard of Paradise and were granted a foretaste of the Kingdom of Heaven. This is our spiritual heritage, and it is ours to call upon in prayer.

Introduction

Every journey, especially in an ancient Christian land as ours, can with prayer become a pilgrimage. A whole family of saints – and often literally a family – hallowed our land of old. Wherever we live, we are never far from places hallowed by these our patrons and protectors. And the places where they dwelt are still potentially hallowed. The blessings that they brought down from heaven to earth are still here, however ugly many places have become through industry, suburbia or mass tourism.

Because of that plot to begin English history half-way through in 1066, many saints are now little known, their holy relics and the churches they built long gone, but the places where they laboured are still here. True, there were many English saints who toiled abroad as missionaries and we no longer can identify their origins. And there are many others whose names and works God has not revealed to us, but this all the more means that England is indeed a hallowed land. The presence of the saints can be sensed even today in the places where they laboured. Feeling their presence in prayer, we can reflect on our destiny as a nation: on the different ages of English history: the first five hundred years when Jew, Greek, Roman and Celt began the hallowing, the second when the Old English continued and deepened this work in what came to be called England; the third, the age of Roman Catholicism, and the fourth the five hundred years of Protestantism. Will there be a fifth age? If there is, perhaps it will be the age of a return to the Christianity of the Old English Church.

The main aim of this book is a pilgrimage to the saints who directly hallowed the English land. For this reason, we do not include here the areas which are historically Celtic, – Ireland, Wales, most of Scotland, Cornwall, Monmouthshire, the Isle of Man, the Scilly Isles and the Channel Islands. However, we do include the Lowlands of Scotland which were until the tenth century part of Northumbria as their English place-names and dialect still testify.

It is impossible to mention every site connected with a saint, every parish dedicated to him (over eighty-three dedicated for instance to St. Cuthbert alone). Nor can we include the hundreds of holy wells in England, nor the names of all the monasteries of the Old English, nor the names of the four hundred or so churches where Old English architecture is visible today. Our interest is in the saints themselves who toiled here in the work of hallowing the land, and the sites directly connected with them of which remains perhaps only a parish church built on the place of an ancient church or monastery.

A special case must be made for some saints and sites. First, Glastonbury, which by ancient but unverifiable tradition was visited by Our Lord and His Holy Mother themselves, and then St. Joseph of Arimathea. Similarly ancient tradition tells that Sts. Peter and Paul visited the land and that St. Paul preached at Ludgate. Also St. Simon the Zealot and then St. Aristobulus, 'Bishop of Britain', visited the land. Finally we cannot fail to mention St. Gregory the Great, 'Apostle of the English', who is widely venerated, even though he never set foot in the land, just as St. George.

Outstanding in the spiritual geography of England are three sites which form a triangle, roughly defining the land: Glastonbury, Canterbury and Lindisfarne, 'Holy Island', which represent respectively the English Jerusalem, Constantinople and Athos the 'Holy Mountain'.

Every county has its saint or saints, except for the then almost uninhabited Westmoreland. The counties mentioned are the historical ones and not the administrative ones of the 1970's. Similarly the dates given are those of the main feasts according to the Julian calendar, which was the calendar of the Old English Church, used indeed right up to the mid-18th century in England. To obtain the civil date of the feast, one must therefore add thirteen days. The date given after each saint's name is the date of the saint's repose, unless otherwise indicated. A brief bibliography is included at the end for those who require details of the lives, parish dedications and sites where Old English architecture is visible.

We believe that, although little is known about many of the saints who hallowed our land, through our unworthy prayers they reveal themselves to us. In this way our forgotten and much-neglected spiritual heritage will be rightfully restored. In the light of this we pray forgiveness for omissions for which through our weakness and sin we are responsible.

All the Saints of the English Land, Pray to God for us!

Fr. Andrew Phillips

Index of Saints

*Indicates that there is more than one saint of this name.

Saint	Place of Pilgrimage
Acca	Hexham, Whithorn
Adalbert	Northumbria
Adamnan	Coldingham
Adulph	Iken, Thorney
Adrian	Canterbury
Aelfric	Abingdon, Canterbury
Agamund	Crowland
Agatha	Wimborne
Agilbert	Dorchester-on-Thames
Aidan	Lindisfarne
Ailred	Bardney, Eastry, Ramsey.
Alban	Minster-in-Thanet, St. Albans
Alburgh	Wilton
Alcmund	Derby, Hexham, Lilleshall.
Aldate	Dyrham, Gloucester.
Aldhelm	Bishopstrow, Bradford-on-Avon, Bruton, Canterbury, Corfe, Doulting, Frome, Langton Matravers, Malmesbury, St. Aldhelm's Head, Sherborne, Wareham.
Aldwyn	Coln Aldwyn, Partney.
Alfreda	Crowland
Alfwold	Sherborne, Winchester.
Alkeld	Middleham
Alnoth	Weedon
Alphege	Bath, Canterbury, Deerhurst, London, Winchester.
Arild	Gloucester, Kingston-by-Thornbury.
Aristobulus	Glastonbury
Arnulf	Eynesbury
Arwald	Isle of Wight
Askega	Crowland
Athelhelm	Canterbury, Wells.

17

Saint	Place of Pilgrimage
Audrey	Coldingham, Ely, Exning, London, Stone.
Augustine	Aust/Aust Cliff, Canterbury, Cerne Abbas.
Aylwine	Athelney
Baldred	Bass Rock, Durham, East Linton, St. Baldred's Rock, Tyningham.
Balin	Lindisfarne
Bede	Durham, Jarrow, Monkton, York
Bega	St. Bees
Begu	Hackness, Whitby.
Benedict	Canterbury, Glastonbury, Jarrow, Thorney, Wearmouth
Beocca	Chertsey
Bercthun	Beverley
Berhtwald	Canterbury, Glastonbury, Ramsbury, Reculver
Bettelin	Crowland, Ilam, Stafford.
Billfrith	Durham, Lindisfarne.
Birinus	Berinsfield, Dorchester-on-Thames, Ipsden, Taplow, Winchester.
Birstan	Winchester
Blida	Martham
Boniface	Crediton, Exeter, Nursling.
Bosa	Whitby, York.
Boswell	Durham, Melrose, St. Boswells.
Botolph	Boston, Bury St. Edmunds, Ely, Grundisburgh, Iken, London, Wenlock.
Brannoc	Braunton
Bregwine	Canterbury
Briavel	St. Briavels
Budoc	St. Budeaux
Caedmon	Whitby
Caedwalla	Wessex
Cedd	Bradwell-on-Sea, Lastingham, Lichfield, Lindisfarne, Polstead, Prittlewell, Tilbury, West Mersea,
Ceolfrith	Gilling, Glastonbury, Jarrow, Ripon, Wearmouth.

Saint	Place of Pilgrimage
Ceolwulf	Durham, Lindisfarne, Norham-on-Tweed.
Cett	Oundle
Cewydd	Lancant
Chad	Barrow, Birmingham, Chadkirk, Chadwick, Lastingham, Lichfield, Lindisfarne, York.
Cissa	Crowland
Clair	Rochester
Clodock	Clodock
Colman	Lindisfarne
Congar	Congresbury
Constantine	Colchester, York
Credan	Evesham
Cuthbert*	Bellingham, Canterbury, Chester-le-Street, Cotherstone, Crayke, Durham, Edenhall, Gloucester, Hereford, Hexham, Kirkcudbright, Lindisfarne, Lyminge, Melrose, Norham-on-Tweed, Ripon.
Cuthburgh	Barking, Wimborne.
Cuthfleda	Leominster
Cuthman	Chidham. Steyning.
Cwenburgh	Barking, Wimborne.
Cyneburgh*	Castor, Peterborough, Thorney.
Cyneswith	Castor, Peterborough, Thorney.
Cynibil	Lastingham
Damian	Glastonbury
Decuman	Dunster, St. Decumans, Watchet.
Deicola	Bosham
Deusdedit	Canterbury, Minster-in-Thanet, Peterborough.
Diuma	Charlbury
Dominica	Glastonbury, Huish Episcopi.
Drithelm	Cunningham, Melrose.
Dubricius	Archenfield, Madley.
Dunstan	Athelney, Baltonsborough, Bath, Canterbury, Glastonbury, London, Malmesbury, Mayfield, Muchelney.
Eadsige	Canterbury

Saint	Place of Pilgrimage
Eanswyth	Folkestone
Eata	Hexham. Lindisfarne, Melrose, Ripon.
Ebbe*	Coldingham, Ebchester, St. Abb's Head.
Echa	Crayke
Edbert	Durham, Lindisfarne, York.
Edburgh*	Adderbury, Aylesbury, Bicester, Castor, London, Lyminge, Minster-in-Thanet, Pershore, Peterborough, Repton, Southwell-on-Trent, Stanton Harcourt, Winchester.
Edfrid	Leominster
Edfrith	Durham, Lindisfarne.
Edgar	Glastonbury
Edith*	Church Eaton, Kemsing, Polesworth, Wilton.
Edmund	Arundel, Attleborough, Bury St. Edmunds, Hellesdon, Hoxne, Hunstanton.
Ednoth	Dorchester-on-Thames, Ramsbury, Worcester, York.
Edward	Brookwood, Corfe, Shaftesbury, Wareham.
Edwin	Edwinstowe, Hatfield Chase, Whitby, York.
Edwold	Cerne
Egbert	Lindisfarne, Ripon.
Egdred	Crowland
Egelred	Crowland
Egwin	Evesham, Worcester.
Elfgete	Crowland
Elfleda	Glastonbury, Hartlepool.
Elgiva	Shaftesbury, Wilton.
Elphin	Warrington
Elstan	Abingdon, Ramsbury.
Elvan	Glastonbury
Elwin	Lindsey
Enfleda	Glastonbury, Whitby.
Eosterwine	Wearmouth
Erkengota	Ely
Erkenwald	Barking, Chertsey, London, Stallingborough.

Saint	Place of Pilgrimage
Ermenburgh	Minster-in-Thanet
Ermengyth	Minster-in-Thanet
Ermenhild	Ely, Minster-in-Sheppey.
Ethelbert*	Canterbury, Eastry, Hereford, London, Marden, Ramsey, Sutton Walls, Wakering.
Ethelburgh	Barking, East Anglia, Lyminge, Wessex.
Etheldwitha	Winchester
Ethelfleda	Romsey
Ethelgitha	Northumbria
Ethelgiva	Shaftesbury
Ethelhard	Canterbury, Louth.
Ethelina	Little Sodbury
Ethelnoth	Canterbury, Glastonbury.
Ethelred	Wakering
Ethelwold	Abingdon, Beddington, Glastonbury, Peterborough, Thorney, Winchester.
Ethilwald	Durham, Lindisfarne, Melrose, Ripon.
Everild	Everingham
Ewald	Northumbria
Felgild	Lindisfarne
Felix	Babingley, Dunwich, Felixkirk, Felixstowe, Loddon, Ramsey, Saham Toney, Soham.
Finan	Benwell, Lindisfarne.
Foillan	Burgh Castle
Fremund	Dunstable, Offchurch.
Frideswide	Binsey, Oxford.
Frithebert	Hexham, Lindisfarne.
Frithestan	Winchester
Fugatius	Glastonbury
Fursey	Burgh Castle
Gerald	Lindisfarne
Grimbald	Winchester
Grimkell	Crowland
Gregory	Canterbury
Gunthild	Wimborne

Saint	Place of Pilgrimage
Guthlac	Crowland, Repton.
Hardulph	Bredon
Hedda*	Lichfield, Peterborough, Winchester.
Heiu	Hartlepool, Tadcaster.
Helen	Colchester, York.
Herbert	Crowland, St. Herbert's Isle.
Herefrith	Thorney
Hereswith	Northumbria
Hethor	Chertsey
Hibald	Bardney, Hibaldstow.
Hilda	Glastonbury, Gloucester, Hackness, Hartlepool, Hinderwell, Whitby.
Hildelith	Barking
Honorius	Canterbury
Huna	Chatteris, Ely, Thorney.
Hwaetbert	Jarrow, Wearmouth.
Ina	Wessex
Indract	Glastonbury, Huish Episcopi, Shepton Mallet.
Ithamar	Rochester
Ives	Ramsey, St. Ives.
Iwi	Lindisfarne, Wilton.
James	Catterick, York.
Janbert	Canterbury
John*	Beverley, Canterbury, Harpham, Hexham, Malmesbury, Whitby, York.
Joseph	Glastonbury
Jurmin	Blythburgh, Bury St. Edmunds.
Justus	Canterbury, Rochester.
Kea	Landkey
Kenedr	Kenderchurch
Kenelm	Clent, Winchcombe.
Kentigern	Caldew, Crossthwaite, Mungrisedale.
Laurence	Canterbury
Lewina	Seaford
Liafwine	Ripon

Saint	Place of Pilgrimage
Lioba	Minster-in-Thanet, Wimborne.
Liudhard	Canterbury
Lull	Malmesbury, Wessex.
Mailduf	Malmesbury
Mellitus	Canterbury, London.
Merewenna	Romsey
Milburgh	Stoke Milborough, Wenlock.
Mildgyth	Canterbury, Eastry, Lyminge.
Mildred	Canterbury, Eastry, Minster-in-Thanet, Tenterden,
Mindred	Exning
Modwenna	Burton-on-Trent, Polesworth, Trensall.
Mydwyn	Glastonbury
Nectan	Hartland
Neot	Glastonbury, St. Neots.
Ninian	Briscoe, Holystone, Whithorn.
Nothelm	Canterbury
Oda	Canterbury, East Anglia, Ramsbury.
Offa	Essex
Osanna	Howden
Osburgh	Coventry
Ostrythe	Bardney
Oswald*	Bamburgh, Bardney, Durham, Ely, Evesham, Gloucester, Kirk Oswald, Lindisfarne, Oswaldkirk, Oswestry, Pershore, Peterborough, Ramsey, Westbury-on-Trym, Winchcombe, Winchester, Winwick, Worcester, York.
Oswin	Gilling, Tynemouth.
Osyth	Aylesbury, Canterbury, London, St. Osyth,
Otger	Northumbria
Owen	Ely, Lastingham, Lichfield.
Pandwyna	Eltisley
Paul	London
Paulinus	Catterick, Dewsbury, Easingwold, Holystone, Lincoln, Littleborough, Rochester, Southwell-on-Trent, Whalley, Yeavering, York.

Saint	Place of Pilgrimage
Pega	Crowland, Peakirk.
Peter*	Canterbury, London.
Plechelm	Northumbria
Plegmund	Canterbury, Plemstall.
Ragener	Northampton
Richard	Hampshire
Ruffin	Stone
Rumon	Romansleigh, Tavistock.
Rumwold	Alstrop, Buckingham, King's Sutton, Romaldkirk.
Sabinus	Crowland
Saxburgh	Ely, Minster-in-Sheppey.
Sebbe	Essex, London.
Sethrida	East Anglia
Sidwell	Exeter
Sigebert	Benwell, Bury St. Edmunds, East Anglia.
Sigfrid	Glastonbury, Wearmouth.
Simon	Caistor, Coverdale.
Swethin	Crowland
Swithbert	Northumbria
Swithin	Winchester, York.
Tancred	Thorney
Tatwine	Bredon, Canterbury.
Tetta	Tetbury, Wimborne.
Thecla	Wimborne
Theodore	Canterbury, Crowland.
Thordgyth	Barking
Thurketyl	Bedford, Crowland.
Tibba	Castor, Peterborough, Ryhall, Thorney.
Tilbert	Hexham
Torthred	Thorney
Tova	Thorney
Trumwin	Abercorn, Whitby
Tuda	Lindisfarne
Ulric	Crowland
Ultan	Burgh Castle, Crayke.

Saint	Place of Pilgrimage
Urith	Chittlehampton, East Stowford.
Walburgh	Wimborne
Walstan	Bawburgh, Blythburgh.
Wendreda	Canterbury, Eltisley, Ely, March,
Weonard	St. Weonards
Werburgh	Chester, Ely, Hanbury, Hoo St. Werburgh, Threckingham, Warburton, Weedon.
Wilfrid*	Brixworth, Canterbury, Evesham, Hexham, Isle of Wight, Leicester, Lindisfarne, Oundle, Peterborough, Ripon, Selsey, Whitby, Wing, Worcester, York.
Wilfrida	Wilton
Wilgils	Northumbria
Willehad	Northumbria, York.
Willibald	Bishops Waltham
Willibrord	Ripon
Winebald	Bishops Waltham
Winewald	Beverley
Wiro	Northumbria
Wistan	Evesham, Repton, Wistow.
Wite	Whitchurch Canonicorum
Withburgh	East Dereham, Ely, Holkham, Ripon.
Wolfeius	St. Benet Hulme
Wulfhad	Stone
Wulfhild	Barking, Horton, Wilton.
Wulgan	Canterbury
Wulsin	London, Sherborne.
Ymar	Reculver

Pilgrim's Guide

ABERCORN (Lothian, Scotland): St. Trumwin, Bishop of Abercorn (c.704). *Feast: 10 February.*

ABINGDON (Berks.): St. Elstan, Bishop of Ramsbury, was first monk here, then Abbot and on his repose (981), was buried here and venerated. *Feast: 6 April.*

St. Ethelwold of Winchester (c. 912–984) was Abbot here. *Feast: 1 August.*

St. Aelfric, Archbishop of Canterbury (1005) was also Abbot of Abingdon. *Feast: 16 November.*

ADDERBURY (Oxon.): St. Edburgh of Bicester (c.650), daughter of the King of Mercia, dwelt here and Adderbury (Edburghbury) was named after her. *Feast: 18 July.*

ALSTROP (Northants.): A holy well dedicated to St. Rumwold (7c.) survives here. *Feast 3 November.*

ARCHENFIELD (Herefordshire): St. Dubricius (c.550) founded a monastery here. *Feast: 14 November.*

ARUNDEL (Sussex): The private chapel of the Duke of Norfolk contains the holy relics of St. Edmund (869). *Feast: 20 November.*

ATHELNEY (Somerset): St. Aylwine (Ethelwine, Egelwine) brother of the King of Wessex, lived as a hermit here and founded a monastery in the 7th century. Prayers addressed to him bring healing to the sick. *Feast: 29 November.*

St. Dunstan (909–988) reformed the monastery here. *Feast: 19 May.*

ATTLEBOROUGH (Norfolk): As a young man St. Edmund (869) is said to have lived here for one year and learnt the Psalter by heart. *Feast: 20 November.*

AUST/AUST CLIFF (Glos.): Almost certainly the site where, as recorded by St. Bede, St. Augustine (c.604) met British bishops in a premature attempt to unite the Church in the British Isles. In commemoration of this meeting the site was thus named after St. Augustine. *Feast: 26 May.*

AYLESBURY (Bucks.): St. Edburgh of Bicester (c.650) was a nun and probably Abbess here where she trained St. Osyth in the monastic life. *Feast: 18 July.*

Holy relics of St. Osyth (c.700) were venerated here. *Feast: 7 October.*

BABINGLEY (Norfolk): Local tradition says that St. Felix (647) sailed here and evangelised the area. The legend says that he was close to the animal world, especially badgers and beavers. *Feast: 8 March.*

BALTONSBOROUGH (Somerset): Birthplace of St. Dunstan (909–988), Archbishop of Canterbury. *Feast 19 May.*

BAMBURGH (Northumberland): Some of St. Oswald's relics were venerated here (642). *Feast: 5 August.*

BARDNEY (Lincs.): Some of St. Oswald's relics (642) were translated here. *Feast: 5 August.*

St. Hibald (7c.) was monk and probably Abbot. His holiness is mentioned by Bede the Venerable. *Feast: 14 December.*

St. Ostrythe, Queen of Mercia, (697), founded the monastery of Bardney and on her martyr's death her relics were enshrined here.

St. Ailred (Ethelred), King of Mercia, (716), gave up his kingship and became Abbot of Bardney. *Feast: 4 May.*

BARKING (Essex): St. Ethelburgh was first Abbess and worked many miracles here just before her holy repose in 675. Sister of St. Erkenwald, Bishop of London, her holy life is recorded by Bede the Venerable. *Feast: 11 October.*

The monastery was founded by St. Erkenwald (693). *Feast: 30 April.*

St.Thordgyth (c.700) was a holy nun here. *Feast: 25 January.*

St. Hildelith (c.712) was second Abbess. She may have been trained in France, knew many saints of the age and was renowned as a visionary and miracle-worker, living to great old age. *Feast: 24 March.*

St. Cuthburgh (c.725), first Abbess of Wimborne, became a nun in Barking. *Feast: 31 August.*

St. Cwenburgh (c.735), St. Cuthburgh's sister, also became a nun here. *Feast: 31 August.*

St. Wulfhild (c.1000) was Abbess of Barking and worked miracles. *Feast: 9 September.*

BARROW (Lincolnshire): St. Chad (672) founded a monastery here. *Feast: 2 March.*

BASS ROCK (Lothian, Scotland): St. Baldred (8thc.) dwelt here as a hermit. *Feast: 6 March.*

BATH (Somerset): St. Alphege (c.953–1012) was Abbot of the monastery before becoming Archbishop and Martyr. *Feast: 19 April.*

St. Dunstan (909–988) reformed the monastery here. *Feast: 19 May.*

BAWBURGH (Norfolk): St. Walstan (1016) was venerated at the shrine here by the simple peasant folk of Norfolk. A holy well existed to him. *Feast: 30 May.*

BEDDINGTON (Surrey): St. Ethelwold of Winchester reposed here on 1 August 984. *Feast: 1 August.*

BEDFORD: St. Thurketyl (887–975), founder of Crowland, a monastery in Lincolnshire, was Abbot of Bedford. *Feast: 11 July.*

BELLINGHAM (Northumberland): St. Cuthbert's well is to be found outside the churchyard wall (634–687). *Feast: 20 March.*

BENWELL (Northumberland): According to tradition it was here that St. Finan (661) baptised St. Sigebert (7c.). *Feasts: 17 February* and *25 January.*

BERINSFIELD (Oxon.): Named after the 'Apostle of Wessex', St. Birinus. *Feast: 3 December.*

BEVERLEY (Yorks.): St. John, Archbishop of York, (721), founded the monastery here and laboured here for the last four years of his life. *Feast: 7 May.*

St. Bercthun (Bertin) was a disciple of St. John and the first Abbot of Beverley, resting in 733. *Feast: 15 May.*

St. Winewald (751) was the second Abbot of Beverley. *Feast: 27 April.*

BICESTER (Oxon.): The relics of St. Edburgh were translated here from Adderbury and venerated (c.650). A holy well was dedicated to her. *Feast: 18 July.*

BINSEY (Oxon.): A chapel and holy well dedicated to St. Frideswide (c.680–735) still survive. *Feast: 19 October.*

BIRMINGHAM (Warwickshire): The relics of St. Chad (672) are kept inside the Roman Catholic Cathedral. *Feast 2 March.*

BISHOPS WALTHAM (Hants.): St. Willibald (c.787), later to be a great missionary bishop in Germany and his brother St. Winebald, later an Abbot in Germany, became monks here. *Feasts:* St. Willibald – *7 July* and St. Winebald who reposed in 761 – *18 December.*

BISHOPSTROW (Wiltshire): Said to be so called from the 'Bishop's tree', i.e. the wooden cross erected here in memory of St. Aldhelm (639–709), to whom the church is dedicated. *Feast: 25 May.*

BLYTHBURGH (Suffolk): St. Jurmin (Germin) (7c.), prince of East Anglia, was buried here and venerated. *Feast: 23 February.*

St. Walstan (1016) was born here. *Feast: 30 May.*

BOSHAM (Sussex): St. Deicola (Dicul) (late 7c.), an Irish missionary, was Abbot of a small monastery and the first to bring the light of Christ to Sussex. *Feast: 18 April.*

BOSTON (Lincs.): Boston is named after St. Botolph (Botolphstone) (680). It may originally have been called Icanho which was the monastery founded by St. Botolph and St. Adulph his brother, though it is more likely to be Iken. In any case holy relics of St. Botolph were venerated here. *Feast: 17 June.*

BOTOLPHS (Sussex): Named after the church of St. Botolph (680). *Feast: 17 June.*

BRADFORD-ON-AVON (Wilts.): St. Aldhelm (639–709) founded a church here, probably on the site of the present Saxon church. *Feast: 25 May.*

BRADWELL-ON-SEA (Essex): St. Cedd, Apostle of Essex (664) built the church of St. Peter, most of which still stands. *Feast: 26 October.*

BRAUNTON (Devon): Probably named after St. Brannoc, a Celtic missionary. A holy well is dedicated to him here. *Feast: 7 January.*

BREDON (Leicestershire): St. Hardulph (7c.) dwelt here as a hermit. *Feast: 6 August.*

St. Tatwine (734), Archbishop of Canterbury, was priest at the monastery. *Feast: 30 July.*

BRISCOE (Cumberland): Holy well to St. Ninian (5c.). He probably evangelised the immediate area. *Feast: 26 August.*

BRIXWORTH (Northants.): St. Wilfrid (c.633–709), Archbishop of York, founded a monastery here, parts of whose building form the present church. Brixworth may have been the site of 'Clovesho' where many Synods of holy bishops of the old English Church met. *Feast: 12 October.*

BROOKWOOD (Surrey): The relics of St. Edward the Martyr (978), King of England, are enshrined in the Orthodox Church here which is dedicated to him. Miraculously recovered, the relics are cared for and venerated by the Orthodox monastic brotherhood and the faithful. A special translation feast is kept on the 3 September as well as the usual *feast* on the *18 March.*

BRUTON (Somerset): It was here that St. Aldhelm built a church (639–709). *Feast: 25 May.*

BUCKINGHAM: The relics of St. Rumwold (7c.) were buried here and a shrine raised to him. *Feast: 3 November.*

BURGH CASTLE (Suffolk): Three Irish missionary saints laboured here in the conversion of East Anglia.

St. Fursey (650). *Feast 16 January.*

St. Foillan (c.655), his brother. *Feast: 31 October.*

St. Ultan (686), a third brother. *Feast: 2 May.*

BURTON-ON-TRENT (Staffs.): This was the spot chosen by St. Modwenna (7c.) for her ascetic struggles, more precisely at Andressey, which was a small, nearby island. Her shrine was at Burton itself, where there was a holy well. *Feast: 5 July.*

BURY ST. EDMUNDS (Suffolk): The monastery was founded here by St. Sigebert (7c.), who entered it to take up the monastic life. *Feast: 25 January.*

The holy relics of St. Jurmin (7c.) were enshrined here. *Feast: 23 February.*

Some of St. Botolph's relics were venerated here after their translation. (680). *Feast: 17 June.*

The relics of St. Edmund, martyred nearby in 869 at the age of 28, were enshrined here. King of East Anglia, he gave his name to the town. Many believe that his relics are still buried somewhere in the grounds of the ruined Abbey and that his holy prayer still protects the town. *Feast: 20 November.*

CAISTOR (Lincs.): Reputed by some to be the burial-place of St. Simon the Zealot in the first century after his martyrdom by crucifixion. *Feast: 10 May.*

CALDEW (Cumberland): A well here is dedicated to St. Kentigern (Mungo). He is said to have used it and other local holy wells for baptising when he evangelised the area. Although he is better known in Scotland, he is in fact 'the Apostle of North-West England'. He reposed in 612. *Feast: 13 January.*

CANTERBURY (Kent): One of the three foremost sites in the spiritual geography of England, we shall list first its Apostles and holy Archbishops. (see Appendix for details).

St. Gregory the Great, Pope of Rome and Apostle of the English. (c.540–604). *Feast: 12 March.*

St. Augustine, Apostle of the English. (c.604). *Feast: 26 May.*

St. Laurence (619). *Feast: 3 February.*

St. Mellitus (624). *Feast: 24 April.*

St. Justus (627). *Feast: 10 November.*

St. Honorius (653). *Feast: 30 September.*

St. Deusdedit (664). *Feast: 14 July.*

St. Theodore (690). *Feast: 19 September.*

St. Berhtwald (731). *Feast: 9 January.*

St. Tatwine (734). *Feast: 30 July.*

St. Nothelm (739). *Feast: 17 October.*

St. Cuthbert (761). *Feast: 26 October.*

St. Bregwine (764). *Feast: 24 August.*

St. Janbert (792). *Feast: 12 August.*

St. Ethelhard (805). *Feast: 12 May.*

St. Plegmund (914). *Feast: 2 August*

St. Athelhelm (923). *Feast: 8 January.*

St. Oda the Good (958). *Feast: 2 June.*

St. Dunstan (988). *Feast: 19 May.*

St. Aelfric (1005). *Feast: 16 November.*

St. Alphege the Martyr (1012). *Feast: 19 April*

St. Ethelnoth (1038). *Feast: 30 October.*

St. Eadsige (c. 1050). *Feast: 28 October.*

Among the other saints of Canterbury, not Archbishops, are the following:

St. Liudhard, Bishop (c.603), chaplain to Queen Bertha of Kent, who predisposed the royal court to the Orthodox Christian Faith. *Feast: 7 May.*

St. Peter (607), first Abbot of Canterbury whose holy relics are still venerated in France at Ambleteuse near Boulogne. *Feast: 6 January.*

St. Ethelbert (Albert), King of Kent, (616), who was the first to accept the Faith from St. Augustine. *Feast: 25 February.*

St. Benedict (Biscop) (628–689) was Abbot of Canterbury for a two-year period in his younger years. *Feast: 12 January.*

St. Mildgyth's relics (7c.) were translated here from Lyminge where she was Abbess. *Feast: 17 January.*

The holy Abbess Mildred (c.700) was translated to Canterbury in the early 11th century. She was St. Mildgyth's sister. *Feast: 13 July.*

Some of St. Osyth's relics were moved here (c.700). *Feast: 7 October.*

St. Aldhelm (639–709) became a monk here. *Feast: 25 May.*

Some of St. Wilfrid of York's relics were translated here. (c.633–709). *Feast 12 October.*

St. Adrian, Abbot of Canterbury, (709), a learned and holy miracle-worker. *Feast: 9 January.*

St. Wendreda's relics were venerated here. (8c?)

St. Wulgan (8c.) was born here and his relics venerated here. *Feast: 3 November.*

St. John of Beverley (721) studied here as a young monk. *Feast: 7 May.*

CASTOR (Northants.): St. Cyneburgh (c.680), foundress and Abbess of this nunnery. To this day a local path is known as 'Lady Cunnybarrow's way'. *Feast: 6 March.*

St. Cyneswith (7c.) succeeded her as Abbess. *Feast: 6 March:*

St. Tibba (7c.) was also linked with the monastic life here. *Feast: 6 March.*

St. Edburgh of Castor, nun. (7c.). *Feast: 20 June.*

CATTERICK (Yorks.): St. Paulinus (644), first Archbishop of York, evangelised this area (*Feast: 10 October*) and was aided by St. James the Deacon (late 7c.) who is *feasted* on the *17 August.*

CERNE (Dorset): St. Edwold (9c.), brother of St. Edmund, dwelt near here as a hermit. A miracle-worker, a monastery was later founded nearby where his holy relics were enshrined. *Feast: 29 August.*

CERNE ABBAS (Dorset): A holy well exists dedicated to St. Augustine (c.604). It is said that he struck the ground with his staff and water sprang from the earth. *Feast: 26 May.*

CHADKIRK (Cheshire): Named after St. Chad (672). *Feast: 2 March.*

CHADWICK (Lancs.): Named after St. Chad (672). *Feast: 2 March.*

CHARLBURY (Oxon.): Missionary-bishop in the area, St. Diuma's relics were venerated here some time after his repose in 658. *Feast: 7 December.*

CHATTERIS (Cambs.): Priest-monk in Ely where he aided St. Audrey, St. Huna (690) lived in ascetic labour at a hermitage just outside Chatteris at a spot now called Honey Farm (Huna's Farm). *Feast: 13 February.*

CHERTSEY (Surrey): St. Erkenwald, Bishop of London (693), founded the monastery here and acted as its first Abbot. *Feast: 30 April.*

The place of martyrdom of the monks Beocca, Hethor and their many companions in 870 when the Danes attacked England. *Feast: 10 April.*

CHESTER (Cheshire): The relics of St. Werburgh, an Abbess of royal family who founded and ruled many nunneries (c.700) were translated here. Greatly venerated by the people for her many miracles, remnants of her shrine survive. *Feast: 3 February.*

CHESTER-LE-STREET (County Durham): The holy relics of St. Cuthbert of Lindisfarne (c.634–687) were brought here to protect them from the Vikings. *Feast: 20 March.*

CHIDHAM (Sussex): St. Cuthman (c.681–8c.) the hermit was born here. *Feast: 8 February.*

CHITTLEHAMPTON (Devon): The church was founded by the holy virgin St. Urith (6c.), who after her martyrdom worked miracles for many centuries here. *Feast: 8 July.*

CHURCH EATON (Staffs.): Holy well dedicated to St. Edith of Polesworth (c.925). Its waters are used for afflictions of the eyes. *Feast: 15 July.*

CLENT (Worcestershire): The place of martyrdom of St. Kenelm (c.821). *Feast: 17 July.*

CLODOCK (Herefordshire): Named after St. Clodock (Clydog) (6c.), a hermit of royal Welsh family. *Feast: 3 November.*

COLCHESTER (Essex): According to ancient tradition St. Helen (c.250–330), mother of St. Constantine the first Christian Emperor and finder of the Cross, was born here. Though some doubt this, it is firmly believed by pious townspeople. *Feast: 21 May.*

COLDINGHAM (Berwickshire, Scotland): St. Audrey of Ely (679) became a nun here. *Feast: 23 June.*

St. Adamnan (680), whose holy life is recorded by Bede the Venerable, was a monk here. *Feast: 31 January.*

St. Ebbe (683) was the first Abbess, a princess famous for her wisdom. *Feast: 25 August.*

St. Ebbe the Younger (870) was martyred here together with her community. *Feast: 23 August.*

COLN ST. ALDWYN (Glos.): Named after St. Aldwyn (early 8c.), who was Abbot of Partney in Lincolnshire. *Feast: 3 May.*

CONGRESBURY (Somerset): Founded by the Welsh missionary St. Congar in he 6c., his relics were later enshrined here and the settlement named after him. *Feast: 27 November.*

CORFE (Dorset): St. Aldhelm (639–709) founded the first church here. *Feast: 25 May.*

The place of martyrdom of St. Edward, King of England, in 978. *Feast: 18 March.*

At the foot of the hill where St. Edward's body was found runs a stream where pilgrims still come to bathe their eyes for healing.

COTHERSTONE (Yorks.): Named after St. Cuthbert (c.634–687). 'Stone' often means 'stone church' in place-names. *Feast: 20 March.*

COVENTRY (Warwickshire): St. Osburgh (c.1018) first Abbess and miracle-worker. *Feast: 30 March.*

COVERDALE (Yorks.): According to a local tradition St. Simon the Zealot was buried here in the first century. There is a similar tradition at Caistor. *Feast: 10 May.*

CRAYKE (Yorks.): Founded by St. Cuthbert (c.634–687). *Feast: 20 March.*

St. Ultan (7c.), Irish Abbot at St. Peter's monastery. *Feast: 8 August.*

St. Echa (767), a hermit famed for his holiness and prophecies. Here he worked miracles. *Feast: 5 May.*

CREDITON (Devon): Birthplace of St. Boniface, Apostle of Germany, Archbishop and martyr, (c.675–754). His original name was Winfrith or Winfred. *Feast: 5 June.*

CROSSTHWAITE (Cumberland): St. Kentigern set up a preaching cross here and the clearing or 'thwaite' was named after it. The parish church is also dedicated to the saint who reposed in 612. *Feast: 13 January.*

CROWLAND (Lincs.): St. Guthlac, father of the fens, hermit and miracle-worker (673–714). He saw the angels and the holy Apostle Bartholomew and lived the ascetic life to the full, having left the princely world of warfare into which he had been born. *Feast: 11 April.*

St. Pega (c.719), anchoress and holy virgin who lived nearby as she was St. Guthlac's sister. *Feast: 8 January.*

St. Bettelin (Bertram) (8c.), hermit and disciple of St. Guthlac. *Feast: 9 September.*

St. Cissa (8c.), also a disciple of St. Guthlac. *Feast: 23 September.*

St. Alfreda (Etheldritha) (c.835), daughter of King Offa of Mercia who had her fiancé King Ethelbert of East Anglia murdered, she lived here as an anchoress and prophetess. Like St. Ethelbert, she too was venerated as a saint. *Feast: 2 August.*

Martyred by the Danes in 870: Theodore, Abbot of Crowland, Askega the Prior, Swethin, Sub-Prior, Elfgete, Deacon, Sabinus, Subdeacon, Grimkell and Agamund, centenarians, Herbert, chanter, Egdred and Ulric, servers and some 70 companion-martyrs. *Feast: 9 April.*

St. Egelred, martyred in the same year, monk, *Feast: 25 September.*

St. Thurketyl (887–975), of Danish origin, he refounded the monastery and became its Abbot. A good example of his people's repentance as they became part of the English Christian Faith. *Feast: 11 July.*

CUNNINGHAM (Ayrshire, Scotland): Once part of Northumbria, it is where St. Drithelm had his vision of heaven and hell as related by Bede the Venerable. He later became a godly monk, reposing in c.700. *Feast: 1 September.*

DEERHURST (Glos.): St. Alphege of Canterbury (1012) became a monk here. *Feast: 19 April.*

DERBY: The relics of St. Alcmund (c.800), martyred prince of Northumbria, were translated here. St. Alcmund (Alkmund) is the patron of Derby and there is a holy well dedicated to him. *Feast: 19 March.*

DEWSBURY (Yorks.): St. Paulinus (644) preached here and baptised. *Feast: 10 October.*

DORCHESTER-ON-THAMES (Oxon.): St. Birinus, Apostle of Wessex (650), first Bishop of Dorchester. His relics were probably venerated here. *Feast: 3 December.*

St. Agilbert, Bishop of Dorchester (c.690). Later, Bishop of Paris, *Feast: 1 April.*

St. Ednoth I, Bishop of Dorchester, martyred here by the Danes in 1016. *Feast: 19 October.*

DOULTING (Somerset): Here reposed St. Aldhelm (639–709). Famous holy well. *Feast: 25 May.*

DUNSTABLE (Bedfordshire): The relics of St. Fremund (866), a hermit of royal origin martyred for his righteousness, were venerated here and miracles occurred. *Feast: 11 May.*

DUNSTER (Somerset): Place of martyrdom of St. Decuman (6c.), a Welsh hermit and missionary. *Feast: 27 August.*

DUNWICH (Suffolk): St. Felix (647), first Bishop of East Anglia. *Feast: 8 March*

DURHAM: The relics of the head of St. Oswald (642) were venerated here. *Feast: 5 August.*

St. Boswell's (Boisil) relics (661) were enshrined here. *Feast: 7 July.*

St. Cuthbert's relics (c.634–687) are still here and venerated by the faithful who ask the prayers of 'the Wonderworker of Britain'. *Feast: 20 March*

The relics of St. Edbert (698),Bishop of Lindisfarne. *Feast: 6 May.*

The relics of St. Ethilwald (699), hermit on the Inner Farne. *Feast: 23 March.*

The relics of St. Edfrith (721), the Bishop who wrote the Lindisfarne Gospels. *Feast: 4 June.*

The relics of Bede the Venerable (673–735) are still venerated here, for they have survived. *Feast: 26 May.*

The relics of St. Ethilwald (740), disciple of St. Cuthbert and successor of St. Edfrith as Bishop of Lindisfarne. *Feast: 12 February.*

The relics of St. Billfrith (8c.), a skilled hermit who bound the Lindisfarne Gospels. *Feast: 6 March.*

The relics of St. Baldred (756), Northumbrian hermit and miracle-worker. *Feast: 6 March.*

The relics of St. Ceolwulf (764), King of Northumbria who abdicated in favour of the monastic life. *Feast: 15 January.*

DYRHAM (Glos.): According to tradition the place of martyrdom in c.577 of St. Aldate, Bishop of Gloucester. *Feast: 4 February.*

EASINGWOLD (Yorks.): Another place where St. Paulinus (644) preached and baptised. *Feast: 10 October.*

EAST ANGLIA: In some cases we do not know the precise origins of a saint, but only the regional origin. Such is the case here:

St. Sigebert, King of East Anglia in the 7c. He introduced Christianity and was renowned for his piety, falling in battle against pagans. *Feast: 25 January.*

St. Sethrida (7c.) became Abbess of Faremoutier in France. *Feast: 10 January.*

St. Ethelburgh (664), sister of St. Sethrida, she succeeded her as Abbess of the holy monastery of Faremoutier. Other sisters of this godly family were St. Audrey of Ely, St. Withburgh of Dereham and St. Saxburgh of Ely. *Feast: 7 July.*

St. Oda the Good (958), Archbishop of Canterbury was also born in East Anglia. *Feast: 2 June.*

EAST DEREHAM (Norfolk): St. Withburgh (c.743), youngest daughter of the King of East Anglia and so sister of St. Audrey of Ely, dwelt here and founded a nunnery. When her holy relics were exhumed, a holy well sprung up which still exists. *Feast: 17 March.*

EAST LINTON (E. Lothian, Scotland): It is said that St. Baldred had a settlement here (8c.). To this day there remains a holy well. *Feast: 6 March.*

EAST STOWFORD (Devon): Birthplace of St. Urith of Chittlehampton (6c.). *Feast: 8 July.*

EASTRY (Kent): Brothers of St. Ermenburgh, Sts. Ailred (Ethelred) and Ethelbert (640) were murdered and buried here. *Feast: 17 October.*

St. Ermenburgh gave birth to three daughters who became saints, Mildred, Milburgh and Mildgyth who succeeded St. Mildred as Abbess of the nunnery. St. Mildred reposed in about 700. *Feast:* (St. Mildred) *13 July,* St. Mildgyth, *17 January.*

EBCHESTER (County Durham): Named after St. Ebbe (683), Abbess of Coldingham. *Feast: 25 August.*

EDENHALL (Cumberland): One of the resting places of the sacred relics of St. Cuthbert (634–687), when they were saved from the Danes. St. Cuthbert's holy well commemorates this event. *Feast: 20 March.*

EDWINSTOWE (Notts.): Named after St. Edwin, King of Northumbria (584–633). *Feast: 12 October.*

ELTISLEY (Cambs.): It is said that St. Wendreda was buried here.

St. Pandwyna (c.904), holy virgin and martyr to whom is dedicated the parish church and a holy well. *Feast: 26 August.*

ELY (Cambs.): Relics of St. Oswald (642) were venerated here. *Feast: 5 August.*

St. Erkengota (c.660), daughter of St. Saxburgh and sister of St. Ermenhild, was linked with Ely, though she became a nun at Faremoutier with her aunt St. Ethelburgh. On her repose, a sweet scent arose from her grave. *Feast: 21 February.*

St. Owen (Owin, Ovin) (c.670) was St. Audrey's steward, a faithful servant who later became a monk at Lastingham. The base of an ancient cross survives to this day in Ely Cathedral. It is inscribed: 'O God, vouchsafe light and rest to Owen'. *Feast: 4 March.*

St. Audrey (Etheldreda) (679), Queen, foundress and Abbess of Ely, England's most loved and venerated woman-saint. She became a nun under her aunt, St. Ebbe, in Coldingham, but founded a monastery in Ely on the site of the present Cathedral. Her left hand can be venerated at the small Roman Catholic church in Ely to this day. *Feast: 23 June.*

The head relic of St. Botolph (680) was venerated here. *Feast: 17 June.*

St. Huna (690), monk-priest, laboured here in the ascetic life. *Feast: 13 February.*

St. Saxburgh, sister of St. Audrey, mother of Sts. Erkengota and Ermenhild, grandmother of St. Werburgh and aunt by marriage to St. Ermenburgh, herself mother of three saints, Abbess of Ely (c.700). In the world as Queen of Kent, she founded the nunnery at Minster-in-Sheppey, to which she retired as Abbess, only then to become Abbess of Ely. *Feast: 6 July.*

St. Ermenhild (c.700), Queen of Mercia, then Abbess of Ely. *Feast: 13 February.*

St. Werburgh (c.700), daughter of St. Ermenhild, became a nun here and then Abbess. *Feast: 3 February.*

The relics of St. Withburgh (c.743) were moved here and venerated. *Feast: 17 March.*

The relics of St. Wendreda (8c.) were venerated here.

ESSEX: King of the East Saxons (Essex) in the 7c., St. Sebbe (694) built the first monastery at Westminster through the intercessions of the Holy Apostle Peter. He himself became a monk and was known for prayer, repentance and almsgiving. *Feast: 29 August.*

St. Offa (c.709), King of Essex, gave up all to go to Rome and take up the monastic life. *Feast: 15 December.*

EVERINGHAM (Yorks.): St. Everild (Averil) (c.700) became a nun here and helped found a very large nunnery of some 80 religious. Everingham may have been named after her. There is a holy well dedicated to her. *Feast: 9 July.*

EVESHAM (Worcestershire): St. Oswald (642) was linked with Evesham, it seems through the translation of some of his relics. *Feast: 5 August.*

St Wilfrid (c.633–709) aided in the founding of the monastery. *Feast: 12 October.*

St. Egwin (717), Bishop of Worcester, definitively founded the monastery after a vision of the Mother of God. The monastery was built on the site of the visions. *Feast: 30 December.*

St. Credan (8c.), Abbot of Evesham. *Feast: 19 August.*

St. Wistan (Winston) (850) had his relics translated here, where they were venerated by the faithful. *Feast: 1 June.*

EXETER (Devon): St. Sidwell (6c.), virgin, was venerated from early times. *Feast: 2 August.*

St. Boniface (c.675–754) became a monk here before his apostolate in Germany. *Feast: 5 June.*

EXNING (Suffolk): Birthplace of St. Audrey of Ely (679). *Feast: 23 June.*

A holy well to St. Mindred (8c.?) exists here.

EYNESBURY (Cambs.): St. Arnulf (8c.?) toiled as a hermit and was venerated after his repose. The town was named after him. *Feast: 22 August.*

FELIXKIRK (Yorks.): In all probability named after St. Felix of Dunwich (647). *Feast: 8 March.*

FELIXSTOWE (Suffolk): Near Dunwich, named after St. Felix who evangelised this area (647). *Feast: 8 March.*

FOLKESTONE (Kent): Grand-daughter of St. Ethelbert of Kent, St. Eanswyth (Eanswitha) founded a nunnery here, almost certainly the first ever in England. Reposing at a young age, her holy relics are venerated in the present parish church, having been revealed in 1885. Her holy repose took place in c.640. *Feast: 31 August.*

FROME (Somerset): A church was built here by St. Aldhelm (639–709). *Feast: 25 May.*

GILLING (Yorks.): St. Oswin (651), King in Northumbria and a godly supporter of the Church was martyred here by pagans. *Feast: 20 August.*

St. Ceolfrith (716), later Abbot of Wearmouth and Jarrow, became a monk at the monastery here which had been built in honour of St. Oswin. *Feast: 25 September.*

GLASTONBURY (Somerset): Glastonbury has a most special place in the spiritual geography of England on account of the ancient traditions which associate it with the beginning of the Christian Faith. According to these traditions, Our Lord Himself walked here and nearby. Other legends relate that the Mother of God sailed here from the Holy Land. Yet others tell of the coming of St. Joseph of Arimathea who planted the famous Glastonbury thorn which flowers at Old Christmas every year. St. Joseph's *feast* is *31 July.* Other saints venerated at Glastonbury include St. Aristobulus, Bishop of Britain, martyred here at the end of the first century (*Feast: 16 March*), the missionaries of the second century, Sts. Elvan and Mydwyn (*1 January*) and Sts. Fugatius and Damian (*3 January*). Other legends connected Irish and Welsh saints with Glastonbury. In Old English times the following saints were certainly venerated in Glastonbury:

The relics of St. Hilda (614–680) were in part translated here. *Feast: 17 November.*

Some of the holy relics of St. Benedict (628–89), Abbot of Wearmouth, were probably translated. *Feast: 12 January.*

The relics of Sts. Indract, Dominica and Companions, martyred in c.700 were venerated especially by Irish pilgrims. *Feast: 8 May.*

Some of St. Enfleda's relics (c.704) were venerated. Like St. Hilda she was Abbess of Whitby. *Feast: 24 November.*

Relics of St. Ceolfrith, Abbot of Wearmouth and Jarrow (716). *Feast: 25 September.*

St. Neot (c.877), hermit, became a monk here. *Feast: 31 July.*

St. Elfleda (936), anchoress at Glastonbury, and much revered by St. Dunstan, to whom she foretold the year and day of her own repose. *Feast: 23 October.*

St. Edgar (943–75), King of England, was buried here. Repenting of a sinful youth, his rule as first King of all England was most peaceful and during his reign some 30 monasteries were founded. He was the father of St. Edward the Martyr. His body was incorrupt and blood flowed from it when examined in 1052. *Feast: 8 July.*

St. Ethelwold (912–984), Bishop of Winchester and great patron of monasticism, became a monk here. *Feast: 1 August.*

St. Dunstan (909–988), Archbishop of Canterbury, was successively monk, hermit and Abbot of Glastonbury. *Feast: 19 May.*

St. Ethelnoth 'the Good' (1038),Archbishop of Canterbury, toiled here as a monk. *Feast: 30 October.*

St. Berhtwald (1045), Bishop of Ramsbury for fifty years and visionary became a monk here. *Feast: 22 January.*

St. Sigfrid (c.1045), Apostle of Sweden, baptiser of the King of Sweden and St. Anne of Novgorod, was a monk of Glastonbury. *Feast: 15 February.*

GLOUCESTER: St. Aldate (c.577), martyr, was probably Bishop of Gloucester. *Feast: 4 February.*

St. Arild (Alkelda) of Thornbury in Gloucestershire, virgin-martyr, was venerated here where miracles occurred at the shrine. *Feast: 20 July*

St. Oswald's body was venerated here (642). *Feast: 5 August.*

Some of the relics of St. Hilda of Whitby were probably translated here. (614–680). *Feast: 17 November.*

Cyneburgh of Gloucester, miracle-worker. *Feast: 25 June.*

GRUNDISBURGH (Suffolk): St. Botolph was buried here immediately after his repose in 680. *Feast: 17 June.*

HACKNESS (Yorks.): As recorded by St. Bede, it was here that St. Begu (660) laboured as a nun., *Feast: 31 October.*

A nunnery was founded here by St. Hilda (Hild) (680). *Feast: 17 November.*

HAMPSHIRE: The native county of St. Richard, a nobleman who died at Lucca in Italy while on pilgrimage to the Holy Land. His relics are venerated there to the present day. This holy man was the father of Sts. Willibald, Winebald and Walburgh (720). *Feast: 7 February.*

HANBURY (Staffs.): St. Werburgh (c.700) is reputed to have founded the nunnery here, where she was buried. *Feast: 3 February.*

HARPHAM (Yorks.): Birthplace of St. John of Beverley, Archbishop of York (721). There is also a holy well dedicated to him here. *Feast: 7 May.*

HARTLAND (Devon): St. Nectan (6c.), a Welsh hermit, was martyred here by thieves, where he had laboured long in the solitary life. A holy well is dedicated to him here. *Feast: 17 June.*

HARTLEPOOL (County Durham): St. Heiu (7c.), first Abbess of Hartlepool. *Feast: 2 September.*

St. Hilda (614–680) was first nun and then Abbess of the monastery, where she succeeded St. Heiu. *Feast: 17 November.*

St. Elfleda (714) was a nun here under St. Hilda before following her to Whitby, where she later succeeded St. Hilda as Abbess, after her mother St. Enfleda. *Feast: 8 February.*

HATFIELD CHASE (Yorks.): St. Edwin, King of Northumbria (584–633) was murdered here. Husband of St. Ethelburgh (Abbess of Lyminge after her husband's murder) and so son-in-law of St. Ethelbert of Kent,

St. Edwin was largely responsible for the introduction of Christianity into the North of England. *Feast: 12 October.*

HELLESDON (Norfolk): Probably the site of the martyrdom of St. Edmund (841–869), King of East Anglia. *Feast: 20 November.*

HEREFORD: St. Cuthbert (758), Archbishop of Canterbury, was first of all Bishop of Hereford. *Feast: 26 October.*

St. Ethelbert (794), King of East Anglia, was treacherously murdered near here and his relics greatly venerated at his shrine in Hereford. Fragments of his shrine remain. *Feast: 20 May.*

HEXHAM (Northumberland): St. Eata (686), Bishop of Hexham, was buried and venerated here. *Feast: 26 October.*

St. Cuthbert (634–687) was briefly Bishop of Hexham before St. Eata. *Feast: 20 March.*

St. Wilfrid, Archbishop of York (633–709), built a church here of which the crypt survives, and a monastery and became Abbot. *Feast: 12 October.*

St. John of Beverley, Archbishop of York (721), succeeded St. Eata as Bishop of Hexham. *Feast: 7 May.*

St. Acca (740), succeeded St. Wilfrid as Abbot of Hexham, and later he became Bishop as well. A builder and adorner of churches, he was also a theologian. *Feast: 20 October.*

The next bishop was St. Frithebert (766). *Feast: 23 December.*

The next and seventh Bishop of Hexham was St. Alcmund (781), who was buried beside St. Acca. *Feast: 7 September.*

The next and last holy Bishop and beloved father of the flock at Hexham was St. Tilbert (789). *Feast: 7 September.*

HIBALDSTOW (Lincs.): Named after St. Hibald, a holy Abbot mentioned by Bede the Venerable. Here he was buried and venerated. *Feast: 14 December.*

HINDERWELL (Yorks.): Named after St. Hilda (614–680) who is said to have had a hermitage here. There is a holy well dedicated to her here which gives its name to the village – Hilda's well. *Feast: 17 November.*

HOLKHAM (Norfolk): It was here that St. Withburgh (c.743) first lived as anchoress. In the Middle Ages Holkham was called Withburghstow, so famous had she become. *Feast: 17 March.*

HOLYSTONE (Northumberland): There is a holy well here dedicated to St. Ninian, Apostle of North Britain (5c.). He is said to have baptised with its waters. *Feast: 26 August.*

St. Paulinus (644) is also said to have baptised here in the nearby stream of Pallinsburn, which is named after him. Here he baptised three thousand in one go. *Feast: 10 October.*

HOO ST. WERBURGH (Kent): Named after St. Werburgh (c.700). *Feast: 3 February.*

HORTON (Dorset): St. Wulfhild, Abbess of Barking (c.1000), lived at the nunnery here and was for time Abbess of Horton as well as of Barking. *Feast: 9 September.*

HOWDEN (Yorks.): St. Osanna (8c?), a royal saint was buried and venerated here.

HOXNE (Suffolk): Said by local tradition to be the scene of the martyrdom of St. Edmund (869), though others claim this to be Hellesdon. *Feast: 20 November.*

HUISH EPISCOPI (Somerset): The place of martyrdom of Sts. Indract, Dominica and Companions (c.700). *Feast: 8 May.*

HUNSTANTON (Norfolk): A headland here is known as St. Edmund's Point. This is where St. Edmund (869) landed on arriving in England. A chapel was later built here to commemorate this. *Feast: 20 November.*

IKEN (Suffolk): This may have been the monastery of Icanho, where Sts. Botolph and Adulph (680), two brothers, laboured in the monastic life. St. Botolph founded the monastery of Icanho which some identify as Boston. *Feast: 17 June.*

ILAM (Staffs): The relics of St. Bettelin (Bertram), patron of Stafford, were venerated at their shrine here and water taken from the holy well dedicated to him. *Feast: 10 August.*

INNER FARNE (Northumberland): See Lindisfarne

IPSDEN (Oxon.): According to tradition St. Birinus (650) built a chapel here to which he would retreat. Its exact site is 'Berin's Hill' which is across the river. *Feast: 3 December.*

ISLE OF WIGHT (Hants.): Sons of a prince in the Isle, Sts. Arwald and Arwald were put to death by pagans on the day following their baptism in 686. *Feast: 22 April.*

St. Wilfrid, Archbishop of York (633–709), was the first to preach here, as far as we can tell. *Feast: 12 October.*

JARROW (County Durham): St. Benedict (628–689) founded St. Paul's monastery here. *Feast: 12 January.*

St. Ceolfrith (Geoffrey) (716) was the first Abbot of Jarrow. *Feast: 25 September.*

Bede the Venerable (673–735) was brought up here and toiled in the monastic life, becoming priest at the age of 30, and wrote his famous historical and theological works here. *Feast: 26 May.*

St. Hwaetbert (c.747) succeeded St. Ceolfrith as Abbot of Wearmouth and Jarrow.

KEMSING (Kent): Birthplace of St. Edith of Wilton (961–984), daughter of St. Edgar, King of England. Famous holy well and ceremony. *Feast: 16 September.*

KENDERCHURCH (Herefordshire): Named after the church of St. Kenedr (Enoder, Cynidr). He was a Celtic Abbot and missionary of the 6c. *Feast: 27 April.*

KING'S SUTTON (Northants.): Birthplace of St. Rumwold (7c.) who was also buried here. He is also called Runwald or Rumbold. *Feast: 3 November.*

KINGSTON-BY-THORNBURY (Glos.): Place of martyrdom of St. Arild (Alkelda) of Thornbury. *Feast: 20 July.*

KIRKCUDBRIGHT (Galloway, Scotland): Named after St. Cuthbert (c.634–687), Bishop of Lindisfarne. *Feast: 20 March.*

KIRK OSWALD (Cumberland): The church of St. Oswald (642). *Feast: 5 August.*

LANCANT (Glos.): Named after St. Cewydd, a Welsh missionary. *Feast: 1 July.*

LANDKEY (Devon): Named after St. Kea, a missionary Bishop, also of the 6c. *Feast: 5 November.*

LANGTON MATRAVERS (Dorset): St. Aldhelm (639–709) founded the church here. *Feast: 25 May.*

LASTINGHAM (Yorks.): The monastery here was founded by St. Cedd (664) who also reposed here and was venerated. *Feast: 26 October.* Holy wells exist to Sts. Cedd, Owen and Chad.

St. Owen (Owin) (c.670) laboured here as monk. *Feast: 4 March.*

St. Chad (672), brother of St. Cedd, he succeeded him as Abbot. *Feast: 2 March.*

St. Cynibil (679), a third brother and priest here. *Feast 2 March.*

LEICESTER: St. Wilfrid (c.633–709) was briefly Bishop of Leicester. *Feast: 12 October.*

LEOMINSTER (Herefordshire): St. Edfrid (675), a Northumbrian priest, founded this monastery. *Feast: 26 October.*

St. Cuthfleda (c.1000), Abbess of the nunnery at Leominster.

LICHFIELD (Staffs.): The relics of St. Cedd (664) were venerated here. *Feast: 26 October.*

St. Owen (Owin) (c.670) toiled here in the monastic life. *Feast: 4 March.*

St. Chad (672), first Bishop of Lichfield. A humble and zealous saint, he founded two monasteries, in Barrow and in Lichfield. His life is described by Bede the Venerable. On his repose his holy relics were venerated at the Cathedral church of Lichfield. *Feast: 2 March.*

Hedda, Abbot of Peterborough (870), martyred by the Danes. Some of his relics were translated here and venerated. *Feast: 10 April.*

LILLESHALL (Shropshire): The burial-place of St. Alcmund (c.800), a martyred prince. Miracles took place at his tomb and the relics were then translated to Derby. *Feast: 19 March.*

LINCOLN: St. Paulinus, first Archbishop of York (644) built a church here. *Feast: 10 October.*

LINDISFARNE (Northumberland): Lindisfarne or Holy Island as it became known on account of its many saints is one of the three main holy places in England, after Canterbury and Glastonbury. The English Athos, among its saints we cannot fail to mention:

Relics of St. Oswald (642) were venerated here. *Feast: 5 August.*

St. Aidan (651), an Irish monk from the Scotland's holy Iona, we was the first Bishop and Abbot of Lindisfarne. St. Oswald founded the monastery hence his veneration, but St. Aidan evangelised the area, taught the Faith. An ascetic, he was model of fasting, poverty and humility. During Lent he would retire to the Inner Farne Island for prayer and repentance. *Feast: 31 August.*

St. Finan (661), also an Irish monk from Iona, St. Finan succeeded St. Aidan whom he resembled in his learning and seal for missionary work. *Feast: 17 February.*

St. Cedd (664) was a monk here and was consecrated bishop by St. Finan, becoming known to history as the Apostle of Essex. *Feast: 26 October.*

St. Tuda (664), Bishop of Northumbria. *Feast: 21 October.*

St. Colman 9676), an Irish monk from Iona, he succeeded St. Finan as Bishop and Abbot. *Feast: 18 February.*

St. Chad (672) became a monk here. *Feast: 2 March.*

St. Billfrith (7c.), hermit who adorned the Lindisfarne Gospels. *Feast: 6 March.*

St. Balin (7c.), prince and brother of St. Gerald who lived the monastic life. *Feast: 3 September.*

St. Iwi (7c.), monk, deacon and disciple of St. Cuthbert. *Feast: 8 October.*

St. Eata, Bishop of Hexham (686) was brought up here by St. Aidan and later became Bishop of Lindisfarne. *Feast: 26 October.*

St. Cuthbert (634–687), Bishop of Lindisfarne and 'Wonderworker of Britain', perhaps the most venerated saint of England. A monk who became a hermit on St. Cuthbert's Isle next to Lindisfarne and then Inner Farne, St. Theodore consecrated him Bishop of Hexham but he quickly moved back to Lindisfarne. He was famous for his miracles, zeal, prophecies and healings. His relics were incorrupt and are venerated at

Durham to this day where they survived the Reformation. Two lives were written soon after his holy repose. *Feast: 20 March.*

St. Edbert, (698), Bishop of Lindisfarne. He succeeded St. Cuthbert and like him spent much time on St. Cuthbert's Isle. Miracles occurred at his tomb. *Feast: 6 May.*

St. Ethilwald (699), monk on Inner Farne. *Feast: 23 March.*

St. Wilfrid (633–709) was brought up at the monastery of Lindisfarne. *Feast: 12 October.*

St. Edfrith (721), Bishop of Lindisfarne, wrote the Lindisfarne Gospels in honour of St. Cuthbert. Successor to St. Edbert. *Feast: 4 June.*

St. Felgild (c.725), hermit on Inner Farne in succession to St. Ethilwald.

St. Egbert (729), who inspired many missions to convert the pagans in Europe, became a monk here before going to Ireland and Iona. *Feast: 24 April.*

St. Gerald (732) became a monk here before emigrating to Ireland where he became Abbot of the English monastery near Inishbofin and founded two other monasteries there. *Feast: 13 March.*

St. Ethilwald (740), Bishop of Lindisfarne and disciple of St. Cuthbert. Successor to St. Edfrith. *Feast: 12 February.*

St. Ceolwulf (c.764), King of Northumbria who abdicated in order to become a monk at Lindisfarne. *Feast: 15 January.*

St. Frithebert (766), Bishop of Hexham, administrated the monastery at Lindisfarne. *Feast: 23 December.*

LINDSEY (Lincs.): St. Elwin (Ethelwin), Bishop, consecrated by St. Theodore. *Feast: 3 May*

LITTLEBOROUGH (Lancs.): It was here that St. Paulinus (644) baptised in the waters of the Trent. *Feast: 10 October.*

LITTLE SODBURY (Glos.): The patroness is St. Ethelina (Eudelme). *Feast: 18 February.*

LODDON (Norfolk): The church here is said to have been founded by St. Felix (647). *Feast: 8 March.*

LONDON (Includes parts of Essex and Middlesex): As the capital, London occupies a special place in history. It was here according to ancient traditions, that St. Paul preached at the Ludgate where now stands St. Paul's Cathedral. It was here that St. Peter by revelation indicated the site of St. Peter's monastery, now Westminster Abbey. St. Peter indeed is said to have preached the Gospel in the British Isles – perhaps it was here in the Roman City of London. Thus the patrons of London are St. Peter (in the West) and St. Paul (in the East). *Feast: 29 June.* Among the other saints linked with London are:

St. Mellitus (624), first Bishop of London. *Feast: 24 April.*

Relics of St. Audrey of Ely (679) are still venerated here at St. Etheldreda's Church in Ely Place. *Feast: 23 June.*

Relics of St. Botolph (680) were venerated at Westminster. *Feast: 17 June.*

St. Erkenwald, Bishop of London (693). Perhaps London's most famous Old English saint, he was consecrated by St. Theodore. Famed for his holiness, he was known as 'the Light of London'. He was buried in the Cathedral of St. Paul and many miracles occurred at his shrine. Bishopsgate is named after him. *Feast: 30 April.*

St. Sebbe (664–694), King of the East Saxons (Essex, Hertfordshire and part of Middlesex including London). The saint abdicated and became a monk. He built the first monastery in the West (the West minster) and was noted for his prayer and almsgiving. He was buried in the old Cathedral of St. Paul and his shrine survived until the Great Fire of 1666. *Feast: 29 August.*

Relics of St. Osyth (c.700) were venerated at St. Paul's. *Feast: 7 October.*

Relics of St. Ethelbert (794) of East Anglia were venerated at Westminster. *Feast: 20 May.*

Relics of St. Edburgh of Winchester (960) were venerated at Westminster. *Feast: 15 June.*

St. Dunstan (909–988) was Bishop of London. *Feast: 19 May.*

St. Wulsin (1002) was the first Abbot of the refounded monastery, called Westminster. *Feast: 8 January.*

St. Alphege (c.953–1012), Archbishop of Canterbury and martyr, was buried in Old St. Paul's. *Feast: 19 April.*

LOUTH (Lincs.): St. Ethelhard, Archbishop of Canterbury (805), was Abbot of Louth. *Feast: 12 May.*

LYMINGE (Kent): St. Ethelburgh (647), daughter of St. Ethelbert of Kent and wife of St. Edwin, after his death she founded the nunnery of Lyminge and was the first Abbess. *Feast: 8 September.*

St. Edburgh (7c.), a holy nun. *Feast: 13 December.*

The relics of St. Mildgyth (7c.) were venerated here. *Feast: 17 January.*

St. Cuthbert, Archbishop of Canterbury (758) was a monk here. *Feast: 26 October.*

MADLEY (Herefordshire): Birthplace of Dubricius (Dyfrig) (c.550), missionary Bishop. *Feast: 14 November.*

MALMESBURY (Wilts.): St. Mailduf (673), Irish monk and founder of the monastery. Malmesbury is in part named after him. *Feast: 17 May.*

St. Aldhelm (639–709), disciple of St. Mailduf, Abbot of Malmesbury and later a bishop. Famed for his learning, he write in both Latin and Old English and many of his works survive. Malmesbury is in part named after him. *Feast: 25 May.*

St. Lull (c.710–786), later Archbishop of Mainz in Germany and learned and holy missionary, became a monk here. *Feast: 16 October.*

St. John the Wise, monk. *Feast: 28 January.*

St. Dunstan (909–900) reformed the monastery here. *Feast: 19 May.*

MARCH (Cambs.): St. Wendreda, patroness and founder of the nunnery here.

MARDEN (Herefordshire): St. Ethelbert (794) of East Anglia was buried here. Also known as St. Albert or St. Albright, there is a holy well in the parish church. *Feast: 20 May.*

MARTHAM (Norfolk): St. Blida (10c.) was buried here. She was the holy mother of St. Walstan of Bawburgh.

MAYFIELD (Sussex): Metalworker's tools belonging to St. Dunstan are conserved in the Roman Catholic convent here. *Feast: 19 May.*

MELROSE (Roxburghshire, Scotland): St. Boswell (Boisil) (c.661), Abbot of Melrose and famed for his holiness, learning and prophecies. *Feast: 7 July.*

St. Eata (686), Abbot of Melrose before St. Boswell and later Bishop of Hexham. *Feast: 26 October.*

St. Cuthbert (c.634–687) was born here in Northumbria and became a monk of Melrose. *Feast: 20 March.*

St. Drithelm (c.700), monk and ascetic recorded by Bede the Venerable. *Feast: 1 September.*

St. Ethilwald (740), later Bishop of Lindisfarne, became a monk here and later Abbot. *Feast: 12 February.*

MIDDLEHAM (Yorks.): St. Alkeld's holy well. St. Alkeld (Alkelda, Athilda) was a woman martyred by the Danes. Two churches are dedicated to her holy memory in the Wensleydale area. *Feast: 27 March.*

MINSTER-IN-SHEPPEY (Kent): Founded by St. Saxburgh (679–c.700). *Feast: 6 July.*

St. Ermenhild (c.700), daughter of St. Saxburgh and Queen of Mercia, mother of St. Werburgh. She became Abbess here before becoming Abbess of Ely. *Feast: 13 February.*

MINSTER-IN-THANET (Kent): Relics of St. Alban (305?) are venerated in the monastery here to this day. *Feast: 20 June.* St. Deusdedit, Archbishop of Canterbury (664) founded this nunnery. *Feast: 14 July.*

St. Ermengyth (c.680), sister of St. Ermenburgh, toiled here as a nun. *Feast: 30 July.*

St. Mildred (c.700), daughter of St. Ermenburgh, was nun and Abbess here, where her relics were and are venerated. *Feast: 13 July.*

St. Ermenburgh (c.700), first Abbess. She was the mother of Sts. Mildred, Mildgyth and Milburgh. Her younger brothers were Sts. Ethelred and Ethelbert. St. Mildred succeeded her. *Feast: 19 November.*

St. Edburgh (751), disciple of St. Mildred and later Abbess of Minster. She corresponded with the great St. Boniface and helped him in his missionary work. She was a skilled scribe and builder of churches. Her relics were much venerated. *Feast: 13 December.*

St. Lioba (782), later Abbess in Germany, became a nun here. *Feast: 28 September.*

MONKTON (County Durham): Said to be the birthplace of St. Bede (673–735). Here also can be found St. Bede's holy well. *Feast: 26 May.*

MUCHELNEY (Somerset): St. Dunstan (909–988)) reformed the monastery here. *Feast: 19 May.*

MUNGRISEDALE (Cumberland): Named after the church of St. Kentigern Mungo (612). The dedication confirms the tradition that this saint evangelised the area. *Feast: 13 January.*

NORHAM-ON-TWEED (Northumberland): The holy relics of St. Cuthbert (c.634–687) were venerated here. *Feast: 20 March.*

The relics of St. Ceolwulf (c.764) were also venerated. *Feast: 15 January.*

NORTHAMPTON: St. Ragener (c.870), martyred by the Danes. His holy relics were miraculously revealed in c.1050 and healings followed, including that of a certain crippled woman, Alfgiva, on Easter Eve. She later became a nun. St. Ragener is said to be the nephew of St. Edmund.

NORTHUMBRIA: Many saints of Northumbrian origin went abroad as missionaries. They include:

St. Wilgils (7c.), father of St. Willibrord, settled here on the banks of the Humber as a hermit. *Feast: 31 January.*

St. Hereswith (690), sister of St. Hilda and nun in Gaul. *Feast: 3 September.*

St. Ewald The Fair and St. Ewald the Dark (c.695), missionary priests and martyrs in Germany. *Feast: 3 October.*

St. Adalbert (c.710), deacon in Holland. *Feast: 25 June*

St. Swithbert (713), Bishop and missionary. Like Sts. Ewald and Ewald his relics survive and are still venerated. *Feast: 1 March.*

St. Ethelgitha of Northumbria, Abbess (c.720). *Feast: 22 August.*

St. Wiro (c.753), monk and Bishop in Holland. *Feast: 8 May.*

St. Plechelm (8c.), Bishop in Holland. *Feast: 16 July*

St. Otger (8c.), disciple of St. Wiro and St. Plechelm. *Feast: 10 September.*

St. Willehad (789), Bishop in Germany. *Feast: 8 November.*

NURSLING (Hants.): It was here that St. Boniface (c.675–754), Apostle of Germany, became a monk. *Feast: 5 June.*

OFFCHURCH (Warwickshire): The royal hermit St. Fremund was buried here after his martyrdom by an apostate and the heathen Danes in 866. He is said to be related to St. Edmund. *Feast: 11 May.*

OSWALDKIRK (Yorks.): Named after the church of St. Oswald (642). When a village is named after a saint, it often means that the parish church is dedicated to the saint because the saint actually lived or was somehow connected with the area during his life. This may be the case here. *Feast: 5 August.*

OSWESTRY (Shropshire): St. Oswald, King of Northumbria (642) was martyred just near here and his relics venerated here. Oswestry means 'Oswald's tree' i.e. Oswald's cross. *Feast: 5 August.*

OUNDLE (Northants.): St. Wilfrid (c.633–709) probably founded the monastery here and later reposed here during the singing of psalms. *Feast: 12 October.*

St. Cett, monk.

OXFORD: St. Frideswide (c.680–735), virgin and patroness. She founded a monastery in Oxford on the site of the present Christ Church, where she is now buried. Part of her shrine still exists there. *Feast: 19 October.*

PARTNEY (Lincs.): St. Aldwyn, Abbot of Partney (8c.) brother of St. Elwin, Bishop of Lindsey, mentioned by Bede the Venerable. *Feast: 3 May.*

PEAKIRK (Northants.): Named after St. Pega, St. Guthlac's saintly sister (c.719). *Feast: 8 January.*

PERSHORE (Worcs.): Relics of St. Edburgh of Winchester (960) were venerated at the monastery which was partly dedicated to her. *Feast: 15 June.*

St. Oswald, Bishop of Worcester (992), refounded the monastery of Pershore. *Feast: 28 February.*

PETERBOROUGH (Northants.): Relics of St. Oswald, King and Martyr (642), were venerated here. *Feast: 5 August.*

The monastery was founded by St. Deusdedit, the first English Archbishop of Canterbury (664). *Feast: 14 July.*

Some of St. Cyneburgh's relics were venerated here. She was Abbess of nearby Castor (c.680). *Feast: 6 March.*

The relics of her sister St. Cyneswith (7c.) were also venerated here. *Feast: 6 March.*

The holy relics of St. Tibba, their kinswoman (7c.) were also venerated here. *Feast: 6 March.*

The relics of St. Edburgh of Castor (7c.), virgin, were also translated here. *Feast: 20 June.*

St. Wilfrid, Archbishop of York (c.633–709), also helped found the monastery here. *Feast: 12 October.*

St. Hedda, Abbot of Peterborough was martyred here with his 84 Companion-martyrs, monks and priests, by the heathen Danes in 870. *Feast: 10 April.*

The monastery was restored by St. Ethelwold (912–984). *Feast: 1 August.*

PLEMSTALL (Cheshire): Named after St. Plegmund, Archbishop of Canterbury (914). He lived here as a hermit and the site was known as 'Plegmundstow' i.e. Plegmund's hermitage. *Feast: 2 August.*

POLESWORTH (Warwickshire): St. Modwenna (7c.), virgin and anchoress, may have founded the nunnery here and have been the first Abbess. *Feast: 5 July.*

St. Edith, Abbess of Polesworth (c.925). She was either the sister of St. Edgar (thus an aunt of St. Edith of Wilton) or else the sister of the great King Athelstan. *Feast: 15 July.*

POLSTEAD (Suffolk): In the village there is a dead oak, the 'Gospel oak', beneath which St. Cedd, Apostle of Essex (664), is said to have preached. A new oak is growing from the old one. *Feast: 26 October.*

PRITTLEWELL (Essex): The church here is said to have been founded by St. Cedd (664). *Feast: 26 October.*

RAMSBURY (Wilts.): St. Oda the Good, Archbishop of Canterbury (958) was first of all Bishop of Ramsbury. *Feast: 2 June.*

St. Elstan, Bishop of Ramsbury (981). *Feast: 6 April.*

St. Ednoth (1016), the martyred Bishop of Dorchester-on-Thames, was Abbot of Ramsbury. *Feast: 19 October.*

St. Berhtwald (1045) was Bishop of Ramsbury for precisely fifty years and famous for his prophecy concerning the end of Orthodox England. *Feast: 22 January.*

RAMSEY (Hunts.): The relics of St. Ailred (Ethelred) and St. Ethelbert, martyred at Eastry in Kent in 640, were venerated here. *Feast: 17 October.*

The relics of St. Felix of Dunwich (647) were venerated here. *Feast: 8 March.*

St. Oswald, Bishop of Worcester (992), Abbot and founder of the monastery of Ramsey. *Feast: 28 February.*

The relics of St. Ives (Ivo) were translated here from nearby and venerated. *Feast: 24 April.*

RECULVER (Kent): St. Berhtwald (731), Abbot of Reculver before becoming Archbishop of Canterbury. *Feast: 9 January.*

St. Ymar (830), monk and martyr. *Feast: 12 November.*

REPTON (Derbyshire): St. Guthlac of Crowland (c.673–714), the fen father became a monk here. *Feast: 11 April.*

St. Edburgh, Abbess of Repton (8c.).

St. Wistan (Winston) (850) was buried here. *Feast: 1 June.*

RIPON (Yorks.): St. Eata, Bishop of Hexham (686) became a monk here. *Feast: 26 October.*

St. Cuthbert (c.634–687) moved here with Abbot Eata and helped start monastic life. Later his relics were translated and venerated here for a time. *Feast: 20 March.*

St. Ethilwald, hermit of Farne (699) was priest-monk here. *Feast: 23 March.*

St. Wilfrid, Archbishop of York (633–709), was Abbot of Ripon and built a church here, the crypt of which survives. Later he was buried here and his relics venerated. There is a holy well dedicated to him nearby. *Feast: 12 October.*

St. Ceolfrith, later Abbot of Wearmouth and Jarrow (716) was priest-monk and baker of the monastery here. *Feast: 25 September.*

St. Egbert of Ripon, Monk (c.720). *Feast: 18 March.*

St. Willibrord (Clement), Apostle of Frisia and Archbishop in Holland (658–739) was educated here by St. Wilfrid after his father had become a hermit. *Feast: 7 November.*

St. Wilfrid II, Archbishop of York (744), reposed here and for a time his relics were venerated here. *Feast: 29 April.*

St. Liafwine (Lebuin) (c.775), missionary in Holland, became a monk here. *Feast: 12 November.*

St. Withburgh of Ripon.

ROCHESTER (Kent): St. Justus, first Bishop of Rochester (627), later Archbishop of Canterbury. *Feast: 10 November.*

St. Paulinus, Bishop of Rochester (644), later Archbishop of York. *Feast: 10 October.* St. Paulinus is the town's patron.

St. Ithamar, Bishop of Rochester (c.660), first English bishop. He took the name of the son of Aaron (Exodus 6,23). *Feast: 10 June.*

St. Clair (Clarus) (9c.), a priest of Rochester who went to Normandy to live the life of a hermit and was martyred. Several places in France are named after him and his name is the origin of the name Sinclair (= St. Clair). *Feast: 4 November.*

ROMALDKIRK (Yorks.): Names after St. Rumwold (7c.). *Feast: 3 November.*

ROMANSLEIGH (Devon): Named after St. Rumon (6c.), an Irish missionary Bishop. *Feast: 30 August.*

ROMSEY (Hants.): St. Merewenna (10c.), first Abbess of the nunnery of Romsey. *Feast: 10 February.*

St. Ethelfleda (Elfleda), disciple of St. Merewenna whom she succeeded as Abbess (c.970). *Feast: 23 October.*

RYHALL (Rutland): St. Tibba (7c.), anchoress and kinswoman of Sts. Cyneburgh and Cyneswith, struggled here in the ascetic life and was buried here before the translation of her holy relics. A holy well exists to her memory here. *Feast: 6 March.*

SAHAM TONEY (Norfolk): According to local tradition St. Felix set a seminary or school here (647). *Feast: 8 March.*

ST. ABB'S HEAD (Berwickshire, Scotland): Named after St. Ebbe, first Abbess of Coldingham (683). The remains of her monastery are still to be seen at this spot. *Feast: 25 August.*

ST. ALBANS (Herts.): Named after the Protomartyr of Britain, St. Alban (305?) who has been venerated continuously since his martyrdom. *Feast: 20 June.*

ST. ALDHELM'S HEAD (Dorset): Named after St. Aldhelm (639–709) who was granted the land of the Head and built churches in the area. It is sometimes called St. Alban's Head by mistake. *Feast: 25 May.*

ST. BALDRED'S ROCK (Lothian, Scotland): This and the nearby St. Baldred's Cradle were named after St. Baldred, the Northumbrian hermit of the 8c., who lived on the Bass Rock near. He is said to have moved St. Baldred's rock by his prayer, since it presented a danger to sailors. Another local geographical feature is known as St. Baldred's Boat. *Feast: 6 March.*

ST. BEES (Cumberland): Named after St. Bega (7c.), an Irish anchoress who lived here and who is mentioned by Bede the Venerable. She is said to have become a nun through St. Aidan and founded a nunnery near Whitehaven. She was greatly venerated in the region. *Feast: 6 September.*

ST. BENET HULME (Norfolk): St. Wolfeius, hermit (c.1000). *Feast: 9 December.*

ST. BOSWELLS (Roxburghshire, Scotland): Named after St. Boswell (Boisil) (c.661),Abbot of Melrose. *Feast: 7 July.*

ST. BRIAVELS (Glos.): Named after St. Briavel (6c.), hermit. *Feast: 17 June.*

ST. BUDEAUX (Devon): Named after St. Budoc (6c.), Celtic missionary. *Feast: 8 December.*

ST. CUTHBERT'S ISLE (Northumberland): See Lindisfarne

ST. DECUMANS (Somerset): Named after St. Decuman (6c.), Welsh hermit and martyr. *Feast: 27 August.*

ST. HERBERT'S ISLE (Cumberland): An isle on Derwentwater, named after St. Herbert (687) the hermit priest who laboured there. He was a close friend of St. Cuthbert and prophesied that they would repose on the same day, which happened. Ruins of a round, stone building on the isle may be those of his cell. *Feast: 20 March.*

ST. IVES (Hunts.): Names after St. Ives (Ivo), a foreign bishop who lived here as a hermit and whose relics were revealed in 1001. A spring of water on the site of the relics had medicinal powers and miracles occurred. *Feast: 24 April*

ST. NEOTS (Hunts.): Named after St. Neot (c.877), hermit in the West Country after becoming a monk at Glastonbury. King Alfred the Great went to him to seek advice and the saint appeared to Alfred on the eve of the decisive battle of Ethandun against the Danes. (King Alfred himself was popularly venerated as a saint for centuries). His relics were translated here in c.972. *Feast: 31 July.*

ST. OSYTH (Essex): Named after St. Osyth (c.700), a princess who founded a convent here, where she was martyred. Her relics were translated for a time to Aylesbury. The original name of St. Osyth was Chich. At. St. Osyth there was a holy well. *Feast: 7 October.*

ST. WEONARDS (Herefordshire): Named after St. Weonard (6c.), a Welsh hermit.

SEAFORD (Sussex): St. Lewina, virgin-martyr (5c.). Many miracles occurred at her tomb. *Feast: 25 July.*

SELSEY (Sussex): St. Wilfrid (c.633–709) founded a monastery here in the course of his missionary work in Sussex. *Feast: 12 October.*

SHAFTESBURY (Dorset): St. Ethelgiva, Abbess of Shaftesbury (896), a daughter of King Alfred the Great, who founded the nunnery. *Feast: 9 December.*

St. Elgiva (c.971), widow of Edmund, King of Wessex, mother of St. Edgar, she retired to the convent to live in piety and charity. *Feast: 18 May.*

St. Edward the Martyr (978), King of England, was venerated here from 980 on. During the Middle Ages Shaftesbury was called Edwardstow, so great was St. Edward's fame. *Feast: 18 March.*

SHEPTON MALLET (Somerset): The relics of St. Indract (c.700) were venerated here. *Feast: 8 May.*

SHERBORNE (Dorset): St. Aldhelm (639–709), Bishop of Sherborne, where he built a church. *Feast: 25 May.*

St. Wulsin, Bishop of Sherborne (1002), remembered for his austerity and simplicity. *Feast: 8 January.*

St. Alfwold, Bishop of Sherborne (1050), famed for his asceticism and devotion to St. Swithin and St. Cuthbert in particular. *Feast: 25 March.*

SOHAM (Cambs.): St. Felix of Dunwich (647) founded the monastery here, where he was buried. *Feast: 8 March.*

SOUTHWELL-ON-TRENT (Notts.): It was here that St. Paulinus (644) baptised in the Trent. *Feast: 10 October.*

The relics of St. Edburgh, Abbess of Repton (8c.) were venerated here.

STAFFORD: The patron of the town is St. Bettelin (Bertram). *Feast: 10 August.*

STALLINGBOROUGH (Lincs.): This is said to be the birthplace of St. Erkenwald, Bishop of London (693). *Feast: 30 April.*

STANTON HARCOURT (Oxon.): The remains of the shrine of St. Edburgh of Bicester can still be seen here. *Feast: 18 July.*

STEYNING (Sussex): St. Cuthman (8c.) toiled here as a hermit, looking after his paralysed mother, and building a church. Here he reposed and was buried. *Feast: 8 February.*

STOKE ST. MILBOROUGH (Shropshire): Named after St. Milburgh (7c.). Fleeing from enemies she miraculously found a spring here, the holy well still exists. *Feast: 23 February.*

STONE (Staffs.): Relics of St. Audrey (679) are conserved at the Roman Catholic convent here. *Feast: 23 June*

Sts. Wulfhad and Ruffin (Rufinus) were martyred here in the 7c. *Feast: 24 July.*

SUTTON WALLS (Herefordshire): Scene of the martyrdom of St. Ethelbert, King of East Anglia (794). The saint is also venerated under the names of Albright and Albert. *Feast: 20 May.*

TADCASTER (Yorks.): St. Heiu (7c.), Abbess of Tadcaster, where she became a nun through St. Aidan. *Feast: 2 September.*

TAPLOW (Berkshire): Another site linked with St. Birinus (650) who is said to have baptised in 'Bapsey Pool', a pond just below the 12th century church. 'Bapsey' is said to be a corruption of 'baptise'. *Feast: 3 December.*

TAVISTOCK (Devn): The shrine of St. Rumon (6c.), an Irish missionary bishop, was here from c.981. *Feast: 30 August.*

TENTERDEN (Kent): St. Mildred (c.700) is the patroness of this town. *Feast: 13 July.*

TETBURY (Glos.): Probably named after St. Tetta, Abbess of Wimborne (8c.). She may have been Abbess of a nunnery here also. *Feast: 28 September.*

THORNEY (Cambs.): The relics of St. Adulph (680) were venerated here, together with some of those of his brother St. Botolph (680). *Feast:17 June.*

The relics of Sts. Cyneburgh and Cyneswith of Castor were in part translated here, together with those of their kinswoman St. Tibba (all 7c.). *Feast: 6 March.*

The relics of St. Huna, monk and priest of Ely (689), were translated here and venerated. *Feast: 13 February.*

The relics of St. Benedict, Abbot of Wearmouth (628–689), were translated and venerated. *Feast 12 January.*

St. Herefrith, monk was buried here and his relics venerated. *Feast: 28 February.*

Sts. Tancred, Torthred and Tova, hermits (St. Tova – a woman) were martyred here by the Danes in 870 and their relics translated to the monastery church. *Feast: 30 September.*

Thorney was refounded by St. Ethelwold of Winchester (912–984). *Feast: 1 August.*

THRECKINGHAM (Lincs.): It seems that St. Werburgh (c.700) founded the nunnery here. *Feast: 3 February.*

TILBURY (Essex): St. Cedd (664), Apostle of Essex, evangelised this area and founded a monastery here. *Feast: 26 October.*

TRENSALL (Staffs.): It seems that St. Modwenna (7c.) founded a nunnery here. *Feast: 5 July.*

TYNEMOUTH (Northumberland): St. Oswin, King in Northumbria (651), was buried here after his martyrdom. His life and work in encouraging the Christian Faith in his kingdom are related by Bede the Venerable. *Feast: 20 August.*

TYNINGHAM (Lothian, Scotland): St. Baldred (8c.) lived here as a hermit, giving his name to nearby places. *Feast: 6 March.*

WAKERING (Essex): The holy relics of Sts. Ethelred (Ailred) and Ethelbert, princes martyred in Kent in 640, were translated here. *Feast: 17 October.*

WARBURTON (Cheshire): Almost certainly named after St. Werburgh (7c.). *Feast: 3 February.*

WAREHAM (Dorset): St. Aldhelm (639–709) built a church here. *Feast: 25 May.*

St. Edward the Martyr (978) was buried here after his cruel murder at Corfe. Holy well. *Feast: 18 March.*

WARRINGTON (Lancs.): St. Elphin, Celtic patron of the town.

WATCHET (Somerset): The patron is St. Decuman (6c.), Welsh hermit and martyr. There is a holy well that never dries up. *Feast: 27 August.*

WEARMOUTH (County Durham): St. Eosterwine (650–686) became a monk here after a military life, no doubt encouraged by his cousin St. Benedict who had founded the monastery. Here he was ordained priest and then Abbot. *Feast: 7 March.*

St. Sigfrid (688) was the second Abbot of Wearmouth and famed for his temperance, obedience and knowledge of the Holy Scriptures. *Feast: 22 August.*

St. Benedict (Biscop) (628–689), founder and then Abbot. He made several pilgrimages to Rome and monasteries in Gaul and was for a brief period Abbot of St. Augustine's monastery in Canterbury. From his journeys he brought back books and icons for his churches, as well as holy relics. He also founded the sister-monastery at Jarrow. *Feast: 12 January.*

St. Ceolfrith (Geoffrey) (716) succeeded St. Benedict as Abbot of Wearmouth, though he was already Abbot of Jarrow. Under him the number of monks increased to 600 and the large library doubled in size. He reposed in Gaul but his holy relics were translated to Wearmouth. *Feast: 25 September.*

St. Hwaetbert (747) succeeded St. Ceolfrith. Renowned for his holiness, letters to and from him survive.

WEEDON (Northants.): St. Werburgh (c.700) seems to have founded the nunnery here. *Feast: 3 February.*

St. Alnoth (c.700), hermit, was martyred in the woods just near Weedon. *Feast: 27 February.*

WELLS (Somerset): St. Athelhelm (923) was the first Bishop of Wells. He was St. Dunstan's uncle and later, like his nephew, Archbishop of Canterbury. *Feast: 8 January.*

WENLOCK (Much Wenlock, Shropshire): St. Botolph (680) was linked with the founding of Wenlock. *Feast: 17 June.*

St. Milburgh (Milborough) (7c.), second Abbess of the nunnery. Princess and virgin, she possessed remarkable healing powers. Her relics healed lepers and the blind; in life she was close to nature and animals. To this day there is a holy well dedicated to her. *Feast: 23 February.*

WESSEX: St. Caedwalla, King of Wessex (658–689), repented of the violence of his youth and encouraged the spread of the Faith. Finally he abdicated to go to Rome where he was baptised with the name of Peter by Pope Sergius. Soon after, still in his white baptismal robes, he reposed in a state of grace. He was one of four Old English kings to repose in Rome. *Feast: 20 April.*

Sts. Ina and Ethelburgh, King and Queen of Wessex (727). King Ina restored Glastonbury and ended his days with his Queen in Rome in piety and repentance. Miracles occurred at their tomb. *Feast: 8 September.*

St. Lull (c.710–786) was born in Wessex but went to Germany as a missionary where he became an Archbishop. *Feast: 16 October.*

WEST MERSEA (Essex): The church here is said to have been founded by St. Cedd, Apostle of Essex (664). *Feast: 26 October.*

WESTBURY-ON-TRYM (Glos.): Founded by St. Oswald (992), Bishop of Worcester. *Feast: 28 February.*

WHALLEY (Lancs.): St. Paulinus (644) preached the Gospel of Christ here. *Feast: 10 October.*

WHITBY (Yorks.): St. Begu's relics (660) were translated here. *Feast: 31 October.*

St. Hilda (Hild) (680) founded Whitby and Hackness and was first Abbess of Whitby. Previously she had been Abbess of Hartlepool where she succeeded St. Heiu and toiled with the encouragement of St. Aidan. Whitby was famous for its learning and produced five bishops and was the site of the Synod of Whitby where the Celts accepted the Orthodox reckoning of Easter. A spiritual mother, both kings and peasants went to her for advice and wisdom. Holy wells exist to her in the area. *Feast: 17 November.*

St. Caedmon (680), first English hymnographer. A simple herdsman, he was gifted by God with writing and singing of the stories of the Old and New Testaments, as is related by Bede the Venerable. He became a monk and reposed in great holiness. *Feast 11 February*

St. Trumwin, Bishop (c.704), a refugee from Abercorn, lived a life of austerity here, where he reposed and his relics were venerated. *Feast: 10 February.*

St. Enfleda (c.704), daughter of St. Edwin and St. Ethelburgh of Kent, she was baptised by St. Paulinus in 626. A widow, she became a nun at Whitby in 670 and later became Abbess. *Feast: 24 November.*

St. Bosa, Archbishop of York (705) was a monk of Whitby. *Feast: 9 March.*

The relics of St. Edwin (633) were translated here under his daughter St. Enfleda. *Feast: 12 October.*

St. John of Beverley, Archbishop of York (721), became a monk here. *Feast: 7 May.*

St. Wilfrid II, Archbishop of York (744), was educated here. *Feast: 29 April.*

WHITCHURCH CANONICORUM (Dorset): The relics of the anchoress and martyr St. Wite are venerated here to this day, having survived intact. Whitchurch is named after her. *Feast: 1 June.*

WHITHORN (Wigtownshire, Scotland): St. Ninian (5c.), Apostle of the Picts. *Feast: 26 August.*

St. Acca (740), Bishop of Whithorn, previously Bishop of Hexham, which was then also part of Northumbria. *Feast: 20 October.*

WILTON (Wiltshire): The relics of St. Iwi (7c.), disciple of St. Cuthbert and deacon, were venerated here. *Feast: 8 October.*

St. Alburgh (c.810) founded the nunnery here and became a nun. *Feast: 25 December.*

St. Elgiva (c.971), nun at Shaftesbury may later have become Abbess of Wilton. *Feast: 18 May.*

St. Wilfrida (10c.), mother of St. Edith of Wilton, repented of a sinful youth and became a nun through St. Ethelwold of Winchester. Later she became Abbess. *Feast: 13 September.*

St. Edith of Wilton (984). Daughter of St. Edgar, she was brought up at the convent and distinguished for her generosity to the poor and familiarity with wild animals. She reposed at the age of 23 and miracles were worked at her tomb. *Feast: 16 September.*

St. Wulfhild (c.1000), later Abbess of Barking, was brought up here. *Feast: 9 September.*

WIMBORNE (Dorset): St. Cuthburgh, Abbess (c.725). Sister of St. Ina, the devout King of Wessex, she became a nun at Barking and then founded Wimborne. She was austere to herself but kindly to others and fasted severely. *Feast: 31 August.*

St. Cwenburgh (c.735) was her sister and also Abbess of Wimborne. *Feast: 31 August.*

St. Gunthild (748), nun at Wimborne at first, she then went to Germany to help St. Boniface and cared for all the schools that had been set up there by English nuns. *Feast: 8 December.*

St. Walburgh (779), nun at Wimborne and then abbess in Germany. Her relics are there to this day and from her tomb flows a miraculous myrrh which heals the sick. *Feast: 25 February.*

St. Tetta, Abbess of Wimborne (8c.). A friend of St. Boniface and a great spiritual mother, she had some 500 nuns under her. Many miracles were attributed to her. *Feast: 28 September.*

St. Lioba (782), a relative of St. Boniface, she became a nun at Minster-in-Thanet and then at Wimborne under St. Tetta. She was one of the 30 or so nuns sent to St. Boniface to help him in Germany, where she became an Abbess. She was a spiritual mother, many of her nuns becoming abbesses in turn and her advice was sought by princes and bishops. *Feast: 28 September.*

St. Thecla (c.790), a relative of St. Lioba, as a nun of Wimborne she was also sent to Germany where she became an Abbess. *Feast: 15 October.*

St. Agatha (790), nun at Wimborne she went to Germany with St. Lioba. *Feast: 12 December.*

WINCHCOMBE (Glos.): The relics of St. Kenelm (c.821), a martyred prince, were venerated here. *Feast: 17 July.*

A monastery was founded here by St. Oswald of York (992). *Feast: 28 February.*

WINCHESTER (Hants.): The relics of St. Birinus, Apostle of Wessex (650) were venerated here. *Feast: 3 December.*

The relics of St. Hedda, Bishop of Winchester (705) are still in Winchester Cathedral. Consecrated by St. Theodore, he was esteemed for his wisdom. Miracles took place at his tomb. *Feast: 7 July.*

St. Swithin (Swithun), Bishop of Winchester (862). One of the best-loved of English saints, he was famous for his charity and church-building. On his repose many were healed by his relics and he is said to help greatly during droughts (hence the superstition of forty days rain after his feast). His relics are probably buried under the shrine in the Cathedral to this day. *Feast 2 July.*

St. Grimbald (c.825–901), monastic and adviser of Alfred the Great. *Feast: 8 July.*

St. Etheldwitha (903), wife of Alfred the Great, she founded a nunnery here and entered it when she was widowed. *Feast: 20 July.*

St. Frithestan, Bishop of Winchester (932). *Feast: 10 September.*

St. Birstan (Beornstan), Bishop of Winchester (934) in succession to St. Frithestan. He loved the poor and prayed much for the departed and himself was rewarded with repose which occurred while he was at prayer. *Feast: 4 November.*

St. Alphege, Bishop of Winchester (951) in succession to St. Birstan. He ordained Sts. Dunstan and Ethelwold. *Feast: 12 March.*

St. Edburgh of Winchester (960) was a daughter of King Edward the Elder and was distinguished for her meekness, remaining a nun all her life. *Feast: 15 June.*

St. Ethelwold, Bishop of Winchester (912–984). Born in Winchester, he is perhaps the greatest of its saints. It was he who instituted the specifically English institution of monastic cathedrals and restored many old monasteries, for example at Milton in Dorset. He would often spend Lent living as a hermit and was an ascetic as well as a builder. A musician, he founded the famous Winchester School of illumination. He even built an aqueduct for the town. He rebuilt the Cathedral and was responsible for its rich liturgy. He is known to history as adviser to the King and 'Father of Monks'. *Feast: 1 August.*

St. Oswald, Bishop of Worcester (992) became a monk here. *Feast: 28 February.*

St. Alphege (953–1012) was Bishop of Winchester in succession to St. Ethelwold, before becoming Archbishop of Canterbury. *Feast: 19 April.*

St. Alfwold (1050) was a monk here. *Feast: 25 March.*

WING (Bucks.): St. Wilfrid is said to have founded and built a monastery here (c.633–709). *Feast: 12 October.*

WINWICK (Cheshire): A holy well exists here dedicated to St. Oswald (642). Some claim that the King was martyred here by Penda, but this seems unlikely. *Feast: 5 August.*

WISTOW (Leics.): Named after St. Wistan (Winston) (850), after his martyrdom here. *Feast: 1 June.*

WORCESTER: Some of the relics of St. Wilfrid (c.633–709) were translated and venerated here. *Feast: 12 October.*

St. Egwin, Bishop of Worcester (717). *Feast: 30 December.*

St. Oswald, Bishop of Worcester (992) and later Archbishop of York. *Feast: 28 February.*

St. Ednoth (1016), the martyred Bishop of Dorchester-on-Thames, became a monk here. *Feast: 19 October.*

YEAVERING (Northumberland): St. Paulinus (644) was active here and in the surrounding area preaching and baptising in the rivers. Part of the Derwent is still known as the Jordan. *Feast: 10 October.*

YORK: It was here that St. Constantine was proclaimed Emperor of the Roman Empire. York is thus also linked with his mother St. Helen and there are many dedications to her of churches and holy wells in Yorkshire. They are *feasted* together on the *21 May.* Apart from this link, York played a special role since its bishops came very rapidly to gain the title of archbishops, assuming a semi-primatial role in the North.

Relics of St. Edwin, King of Northumbria (584–633), were venerated here after their translation. *Feast: 12 October.*

St. Paulinus (644), first Archbishop of York, most active in preaching and baptising in the rivers and streams all over the North. His life and appearance are described by Bede the Venerable. *Feast: 10 October.*

St. Chad, Archbishop of York (672). *Feast: 2 March.*

St. James, deacon (late 7c.). *Feast: 17 August.*

St. Bosa, Archbishop of York (705). *Feast: 9 March.*

St. Wilfrid, Archbishop of York (c.633–709). Although lacking tact and diplomacy, St. Wilfrid was perhaps the most energetic of all York's bishops. He was intensely aware that the Church needed close links with the rulers of the time. He was most active in missionary work in the North, the Midlands, Sussex and Frisia, where he more or less initiated the great English missions to the Continent which were to bring the light of Christ to virtually all north-west Europe. It is most unhappy that the fruits of these missions were later to fall under the control of semi-barbarians like Charlemagne who introduced the filioque that would eventually, under Norman influence, take over the English Church in turn and distort the Orthodox Faith. *Feast: 12 October.*

St. John of Beverley, Archbishop of York (721). He succeeded St. Bosa and was of the same spirit as St. Cuthbert. He loved the poor and cared for the handicapped. It was he who ordained Bede the Venerable both deacon and priest. *Feast: 7 May.*

The relics of Bede the Venerable (673–735) were venerated here for a time. *Feast: 26 May.*

St. Wilfrid II, Archbishop of York. *Feast: 29 April.*

St. Edbert (768), successor of St. Ceolwulf as King of Northumbria, he abdicated after a successful reign and spent the last ten years of his life in monasticism in York. *Feast: 20 August.*

St. Willehad (789) was educated at York and later became bishop in Germany, after several years in Holland as a missionary. *Feast: 8 November.*

St. Oswald. Archbishop of York (992). An ascetic and much loved for his charity, he reposed while reciting the psalms. Of the same spirit as St. Swithin, together with St. Dunstan and St. Ethelwold he was one of the great three bishops in England's religious and so cultural reawakening of the tenth century. *Feast: 28 February.*

St. Ednoth (1016), martyred Bishop of Dorchester-on-Thames, was probably a monk in York. *Feast: 19 October.*

The Patriarchs of the English Church

In just three years from now we shall be celebrating the 1400th anniversary of the Baptism of the English people, the beginning of a 450 year period when the English Church was in communion with the Orthodox East on account of its confession of the Orthodox Faith. During that whole period the most important place was surely Canterbury, the English Constantinople or, if you prefer, the English Kiev, the Mother-City or Metropolis of the English Church. And the most important figures of that period are surely the 35 Archbishops of Canterbury and above all 22 of them who were venerated either locally or else nationally as saints. That two-thirds of the head-bishops of the English Church lived holy lives is all the more remarkable when one considers that the Roman Catholic period of the national Church produced only three Roman Catholic saints – and those in the immediate post-Schism period of the eleventh to thirteenth centuries.

But who were these 22 Archbishops, to whom, on account of their holiness, we might be permitted to give the title of 'Patriarchs of the English Church'?

Augustine (Austin), the First Archbishop of Canterbury and Apostle of the English. (597–c.604). Full details of his missionary work are described by Bede the Venerable in his 'History of the English Church and People'. Almost certainly from Sicily or the South of Italy, he was sent by St. Gregory the Great (the Dialogist) who is also called 'Apostle of the English'. In his very short episcopate he was able to found the Church among the English and in particular convert the Kingdom of Kent. *Feast: 26 May.*

Laurence, second Archbishop. (c.604–619). St. Laurence was also Italian, perhaps a Roman, and was able through the intervention of the Holy Apostle Peter to consolidate St. Augustine's work, as is related by Bede the Venerable. This is not the only case of the intervention of the Holy Apostle in English history, for he is said to have preached in Roman Britannia. St. Laurence's tomb still exists and was opened at the beginning of the century. *Feast: 3 February.*

Mellitus, third Archbishop. (619–624). Also a Roman, though bearing a Greek name, he came to England in 601 as an Abbot. In 604 he was consecrated by St. Augustine as first Bishop of London, where a church had been built dedicated to St. Paul, who was also said to have preached in London. This church has been rebuilt a number of times, is located on the very site where St. Paul is said to have preached and is still called 'St. Paul's Cathedral'. Mellitus, however, was expelled soon after for his refusal to give communion ('white bread', as the unbaptised called it) to unbaptised. Nevertheless he served the Church in Canterbury, becoming its Archbishop and like St. Augustine worked miracles. *Feast: 24 April.*

Justus, fourth Archbishop. (624–627). From Italy, he arrived with St. Mellitus and in 604 became the first Bishop of Rochester. He was buried like the other holy Archbishops in St. Augustine's Monastery in Canterbury. *Feast: 10 November.*

Honorius, fifth Archbishop. (627–653). Arriving in 601, he was consecrated in Lincoln. He greatly strengthened missionary work and made the Roman mission to the English truly national, encouraging the Celtic St. Aidan in Northumbria, the Burgundian St. Felix in East Anglia, the Lombard St. Birinus in Wessex and the Frank Agilbert (later Bishop of Paris) also in Wessex. From his time one can speak of a national Church and the beginning of a sense of national consciousness and even unity. *Feast: 30 September.*

Deusdedit (Frithona), sixth Archbishop. (655–664). No doubt St. Honorius who did so much to organise a national Church was active in preparing this first English Archbishop for his task. He took the name 'Deusdedit', meaning 'dedicated to God'. He founded monasteries in Peterborough and the isle of Thanet and consecrated Damian Bishop of Rochester. His relics were venerated at his shrine until the destruction of the Reformation. *Feast: 14 July.*

Theodore, eighth Archbishop. (668–690). Certainly one of the greatest of all the saints of England, he was a Greek from Tarsus, the City of St. Paul. A monk by choice and also highly educated, he passed rapidly through all the clerical orders at the age of 65. Despite his age he was immensely dynamic and travelled all over England. He founded a seminary in Canterbury where Greek was taught to a high level, consecrated bishops, organised dioceses and above all united the Roman and Celtic branches of Orthodoxy in the British Isles. In this way the conversion of the English was completed and the English themselves were able to go out and convert the pagan peoples of north-western Europe, working together with the Irish missionaries, thus bringing salvation to tens of thousands of souls. St. Theodore organised synods of the whole English Church and in particular maintained the Orthodoxy of the Church against the Monothelite heresy. St. Theodore's body was incorrupt, the symbol of a golden age of holiness in the English Church, for which St. Theodore by the grace of God was largely responsible. *Feast: 19 September.*

Berhtwald (Beorhtweald), ninth Archbishop. (693–731). Abbot of Reculver and most learned in the Scriptures, he was consecrated in Lyons. He continued the work of St. Theodore and corresponded with the great English saints of the age, Aldhelm, Boniface and Wilfrid. *Feast: 9 January.*

Tatwine, tenth Archbishop. (731–734). Firstly monk at the monastery of Bredon in Leicestershire, he was famed for his piety and learning. *Feast: 30 July.*

Nothelm, eleventh Archbishop. (735–739). A learned priest of the diocese of London, he helped Bede the Venerable compile his work on the English Church. He corresponded with the English St. Boniface, Apostle of Germany. Like his predecessor, his episcopate was short but full, and like him he was venerated in Canterbury. *Feast: 17 October.*

Cuthbert, twelfth Archbishop. (c.740–761). A monk at Lyminge in Kent, then Bishop of Hereford, St. Cuthbert did much to encourage the English missions in Europe. *Feast: 26 October.*

Bregwine, thirteenth Archbishop. (761–764). Almost certainly of German origin, he had come to England to study at the seminary-school founded by St. Theodore. He was closely linked, for obvious reasons, with the English missionaries in Germany. Like St. Cuthbert he was buried and then venerated in Canterbury Cathedral itself. *Feast: 24 August.*

Janbert (Jaenbeorht), fourteenth Archbishop. (765–792). From Kent, he received his monastic training at the monastery of St. Augustine in Canterbury, where he became Abbot. His greatest feat was to stand up to

King Offa of Mercia who through his huge power wished to obtain total control over the Church, and styled himself on the tyrannical Continental 'Emperor', Charlemagne. *Feast: 12 August.*

Ethelhard (Aethelheard), fifteenth Archbishop. (793–805). First of all Abbot of Louth in Lincolnshire, he suffered much from the rivalry between the Mercians ruled by King Offa and the people of Kent. At a synod of the English Church in 803, St. Ethelhard established the custom of making every new bishop give a written confession of his Orthodoxy. The fifteenth Archbishop of Canterbury and its fourteenth saint, St. Ethelhard was much venerated in Canterbury until the Normans who attempted to suppress the veneration of many Old English saints. *Feast: 12 May.*

Plegmund, twentieth Archbishop. (890–914). Consecrated at the end of the disastrous ninth century during which the Vikings had all but destroyed monastic life and literacy, St. Plegmund was one of the restorers of the Old English church. St. Plegmund was first a hermit on an island in Cheshire, where he came from. He gave his name to the island which was called Plegmundstow, or today Plemstall, meaning 'Plegmund's hermitage'. St. Plegmund's piety and learning was used by Alfred the Great, who had saved England from heathenism militarily and was now set on saving it spiritually. St. Plegmund helped translate St. Gregory the Great's 'Pastoral Care' into Old English and took part in other like activities. In 901 he crowned Edward the Elder, in 908 he founded the New Minster in Winchester and was extremely active in re-organising the church, consecrating seven bishops on one single day for old and new dioceses. His work was to lead to the second golden age of the Old English Church in the tenth century. *Feast: 2 August.*

Athelhelm (Athelm), twenty-first Archbishop. (914–923). This saint continued the work of his predecessor in restoring church life. He was first Bishop of Wells and almost certainly came from the West country. He was also the uncle of St. Dunstan, and to some extent inspired him in childhood, inviting him as a child to Canterbury. St. Athelhelm also helped prepare Athelstan, grandson of Alfred the Great, who was to become one of England's greatest kings. *Feast: 8 January.*

Oda the Good, twenty third Archbishop. (942–958). Born in East Anglia but of Danish origin, he was first of all Bishop of Ramsbury in Wiltshire and was a skilled and trusted advisor to King Athelstan who reconquered England from Viking settlers, as he was to the King's successors. He himself had become a monk in France and he encouraged St. Dunstan to reorganise monastic life and encouraged his own nephew, Oswald, who was to become the great Archbishop of York. St Oda received the title of 'the Good' for his tireless efforts to revive the English church in many pastoral activities. He was a model Archbishop and famed for his miracles. *Feast: 2 June.*

Dunstan, twenty-sixth Archbishop. (960–988). St. Dunstan ruled the English Church during probably its greatest period, a golden age for which he was in part responsible. Born in c.909 at Baltonsborough near Glastonbury, his family was a noble one and linked to the royal family. He was educated at the ancient and holy monastery of Glastonbury, went to Canterbury and the court of King Athelstan. Here he was expelled after being slandered by those jealous of his gifts. He was then ordained by St. Alphege, Bishop of Winchester and returned to Glastonbury as a hermit where he practised manual crafts. At the age of 30 be became Abbot of Glastonbury. This was the beginning of the restoration of monastic life throughout England. To do this after the Viking invasions he had first to overcome the opposition of rich local magnates who did not wish to lose land, wealth and power to the Church. At the age of 46 the saint was exiled to Flanders but was soon to return, called back by St. Edgar the Peaceful, the first King of All England. In 957 Dunstan became Bishop of Worcester, in 959 Bishop of London and then in 960 Archbishop. He reformed six monasteries personally and protected monasteries from the magnates by close co-operation with royal power. This was a period of symphony between Church and State. St. Dunstan insisted on fasting and its importance, rebuilt churches, renewed monasticism and rewrote the coronation service, which has not substantially changed since. St. Dunstan educated St. Edward the Martyr who was murdered for his patronage of monasticism, and St. Dunstan encouraged the veneration of the martyr. The saint was also a visionary and prophesied the evils that were to follow the martyrdom of St. Edward, including ultimately the Norman invasion. He worked miracles and was most devoted to the Canterbury saints, especially St. Oda the Good. His veneration was nationwide. *Feast: 19 May.*

Aelfric, twenty-ninth Archbishop. (995–1005). Abbot of Abingdon in Berkshire, St. Aelfric was distinguished for his holiness and his leadership during the critical time of the Danish invasion of Kent. Bishop of Wilton immediately before becoming Archbishop, after his repose he was much venerated in Canterbury. *Feast: 16 November.*

Alphege (Aelfheah) the Martyr, thirtieth Archbishop. (1005–1012). A monk at Deerhurst in Gloucestershire and then a hermit in Somerset, St. Alphege became Abbot of Bath. In 984, at the age of 31, he was consecrated Bishop of Winchester, where he was known for his almsgiving and personal asceticism. In September 1011, already Archpastor of the nation, he was taken prisoner by the Danes after they had besieged and then captured Canterbury. They demanded a huge ransom for the Archbishop which the Archbishop refused to pay and forbade others to pay. Furious, the Danes murdered him at a drunken feast at Greenwich. The saint was buried in St. Paul's Cathedral in London and became a national saint and hero. In 1023 his holy relics were translated to Canterbury where they were much venerated and later found to be incorrupt. St. Alphege is the only Orthodox Archbishop of Canterbury to be a martyr. *Feast: 19 April.*

Ethelnoth (Ednoth), thirty-second Archbishop. (1020–1038). A monk of Glastonbury, the saint was chief counsellor to King Cnut. The seventh monk of Glastonbury to become Archbishop, he was famed for his wisdom and reposed much revered, earning the title of 'the Good'. *Feast: 30 October.*

Eadsige, thirty-third Archbishop. (1038–c.1050). The last canonical English Archbishop before the Norman invasion and the Schism of 1054, St. Eadsige crowned Edward the Confessor, so restoring the English line. A patriot, it seems that he gave up his See somewhat before his holy repose. *Feast: 28 October.*

May this brief enumeration be of inspiration to us. Let us note how many were hermits, true monks but also national leaders, even though by no means even English. Perhaps we could add the following intercession to our daily prayers:

Holy Archpastors, Augustine, Laurence, Mellitus, Justus, Honorius, Deusdedit, Theodore, Berhtwald, Tatwine, Nothelm, Cuthbert, Bregwin, Janbert, Ethelhard, Plegmund, Athelhelm, Oda, Dunstan, Aelfric, Alphege, Ethelnoth and Eadsige, pray to God for the salvation of the English land and people!

Julian Calendar of Saints

There follows a Julian calendar of Old English saints and others who worked for the hallowing of the English land. Included are a number of saints not given in the Pilgrim's Guide. They are mainly missionaries who laboured outside England. They are marked with an asterisk *.

JANUARY

01	Elvan and Mydwyn, Missionaries
03	Fugatius and Damian, Missionaries
06	Peter, Abbot of Canterbury
07	Brannoc of Braunton, Monk
08	Ethelbert, Bishop in Ireland *
	Pega, Anchoress
	Athelhelm, Archbishop of Canterbury
	Wulsin, Bishop of Sherborne
09	Adrian, Abbot of Canterbury
	Berhtwald, Archbishop of Canterbury
10	Sethrida, Abbess in France
12	Benedict, Abbot of Wearmouth
13	Kentigern (Mungo), Apostle of North-West England
15	Ceolfwulf, King of Northumbria, Monk
16	Fursey of East Anglia, Missionary
17	Mildgyth, Virgin
18	Wilfrid, Missionary and Martyr in Sweden *
22	Berhtwald, Bishop of Ramsbury
25	Sigebert, King of East Anglia, Martyr
	Thordgyth of Barking, Nun
28	John the Wise of Malmesbury
30	Bathild of Chelles, Queen *
31	Adamnan of Coldingham, Monk
	Wilgils, Hermit

FEBRUARY

03	Laurence, Archbishop of Canterbury
	Werburgh of Chester, Abbess
04	Aldate, Bishop of Gloucester and Martyr
	Liephard, Bishop and Martyr in France *
07	Richard, Confessor
08	Elfleda, Abbess of Whitby
	Cuthman of Steyning, Hermit
10	Merewenna, Abbess of Romsey
	Trumwin, Bishop of Abercorn
11	Caedmon of Whitby, Monk and Hymnographer
12	Ethilwald, Bishop of Lindisfarne
13	Huna of Ely, Priest and Hermit
	Ermenhild, Abbess of Ely
15	Sigfrid, Apostle of Sweden
17	Finan, Bishop of Lindisfarne
18	Colman, Bishop of Lindisfarne
	Ethelina of Gloucestershire
21	Erkengota, Virgin
23	Jurmin of East Anglia, Confessor
	Milburgh, Abbess of Wenlock
25	Ethelbert, King of Kent
	Walburgh the Myrrh-Giver, Abbess
27	Alnoth of Stowe, Martyr
28	Herefrith, Monk
	Oswald, Bishop of Worcester

MARCH

01	Swithbert the Elder, Bishop of the Frisians
02	Chad, Bishop of Lichfield
	Cynibil, Confessor
04	Owen of Lichfield, Hermit
06	Cyneburgh and Cyneswith, Abbesses of Castor and Tibba, Anchoress
	Baldred and Billfrith, Hermits
07	Eosterwine, Abbot of Wearmouth

MARCH (continued)

08	Felix, Bishop of Dunwich
09	Bosa, Archbishop of York
12	Gregory the Great, Pope of Rome and Apostle of the English
	Alphege the Elder, Bishop of Winchester
13	Gerald of Mayo, Abbot
16	Aristobulus the Holy Apostle, Bishop of Britain
17	Withburgh of Dereham, Virgin
18	Egbert of Ripon, Confessor
	Edward the Martyr, King of England
19	Alcmund, Martyr
20	Cuthbert, Bishop of Lindisfarne and Wonderworker of Britain
	Herbert of Derwentwater, Hermit
23	Ethilwald of Farne, Hermit
24	Hildelith, Abbess of Barking
25	Alfwold, Bishop of Sherborne
27	Alkeld, Martyr in Yorkshire
30	Osburgh, Abbess of Coventry

APRIL

01	Agilbert, Bishop of Dorchester-on-Thames
06	Elstan, Bishop of Ramsbury
09	Theodore, Abbot of Crowland and his Companion-Martyrs
10	Beocca, Hethor and Companions, Martyrs under the Danes
	Hedda, Abbot of Peterborough
11	Guthlac of Crowland, Hermit and Wonderworker
12	Wigbert, Monk and Missionary *
18	Deicola, Abbot of Bosham
19	Alphege the Martyr, Archbishop of Canterbury
20	Caedwalla, King of Wessex
22	Arwald and Arwald, Martyrs
24	Mellitus, Archbishop of Canterbury
	Egbert of Ireland, Bishop
	Ives of Huntingdonshire, Bishop and Hermit
27	Kenedr, Missionary
	Winewald, Abbot of Beverley

APRIL (continued)

29	Wilfrid the Younger, Archbishop of York
	Swithbert the Younger, Bishop and Missionary *
30	Erkenwald, Bishop of London

MAY

02	Ultan, Missionary in East Anglia
03	Elwin, Bishop of Lindsey
	Aldwyn, Abbot of Partney
	Philip, Hermit *
04	Ailred, Abbot of Bardney
05	Echa of Crayke, Hermit
06	Edbert, Bishop of Lindisfarne
07	Liudhard of Canterbury, Bishop
	John of Beverley, Archbishop of York
08	Indract, Dominica and Companion-Martyrs
	Wiro, Bishop and Missionary
10	Simon the Zealot
11	Fremund of Offchurch, Martyr
12	Ethelhard, Archbishop of Canterbury
15	Bercthun, Abbot of Beverley
17	Mailduf, Abbot of Malmesbury
18	Elgiva of Shaftesbury, Widow
19	Dunstan, Archbishop of Canterbury
20	Ethelbert, King of East Anglia, Martyr
21	Helen, mother of Constantine, Emperor of the Roman Empire
25	Aldhelm, Bishop of Sherborne
26	Augustine, Archbishop of Canterbury and Apostle of the English
	Bede the Venerable
30	Walstan of Bawburgh, Confessor

JUNE

01	Wite of Dorset, Anchoress and Martyr
	Wistan of Evesham, Martyr
02	Oda the Good, Archbishop of Canterbury
04	Edfrith, Bishop of Lindisfarne

JUNE (continued)

05	Boniface of Crediton, Apostle and Patron-Saint of Germany and his 52 Companion-Martyrs
10	Ithamar, Bishop of Rochester
11	Herebald, Hermit in Brittany *
15	Edburgh of Winchester, Virgin
17	Nectan, Hermit and Martyr
	Briavel, Hermit
	Botolph and Adulf, Confessors
20	Alban of Verulamium, Protomartyr of Britain
	Edburgh of Castor, Virgin
21	Engelmund, Abbot and Missionary *
23	Audrey, Abbess of Ely
25	Adalbert of Egmond, Archdeacon and Missionary *
	Cyneburgh of Gloucester, Martyr
29	Peter and Paul, Holy Apostles.

JULY

01	Cewydd, Hermit
02	Swithin, Bishop of Winchester, Wonderworker
05	Modwenna of Burton, Anchoress
06	Saxburgh, Abbess of Ely
07	Ethelburgh of Faremoutier, Abbess
	Boswell, Abbot of Melrose
	Hedda, Bishop of Winchester
	Willibald, Bishop and Missionary
08	Urith of Chittlehampton, Virgin-Martyr
	Grimbald, Monk
	Edgar the Peaceful, King of England
09	Everild, Abbess of Everingham
11	Amabilis, Virgin *
	Thurketyl, Abbot of Crowland
13	Mildred, Abbess of Minster-in-Thanet
14	Deusdedit, Archbishop of Canterbury
	Marchelm, Missionary *
15	Edith, Abbess of Polesworth

JULY (continued)

16	Plechelm, Missionary and Bishop
17	Kenelm, Martyr
18	Edburgh and Edith, Virgins
20	Arild of Gloucestershire, Virgin-Martyr
	Etheldwitha of Winchester, Widow
24	Christiana, Virgin *
	Wulfhad and Ruffin, Martyrs
25	Lewina, Virgin-Martyr
28	Ardwin, Gerald, Fulk and Bernard, Confessors *
30	Ermengyth of Thanet, Virgin
	Tatwine, Archbishop of Canterbury
31	Neot, Hermit
	Joseph of Arimathea

AUGUST

01	Ethelwold, Bishop of Winchester and Father of Monks
02	Sidwell, Virgin-Martyr
	Alfreda of Crowland, Virgin
	Plegmund, Archbishop of Canterbury
05	Oswald, King and Martyr
06	Hardulph, Hermit
08	Ultan, Abbot of Crayke
10	Bettelin of Stafford, Hermit
12	Janbert, Archbishop of Canterbury
13	Wigbert, Abbot and Missionary *
14	Werenfrid, Missionary *
17	James the Deacon of York
19	Credan, Abbot of Evesham
20	Oswin, King and Martyr
	Edbert of York, Monk
22	Sigfrid, Abbot of Wearmouth
	Ethelgitha of Northumbria, Abbess
	Arnulf of Eynesbury, Hermit
23	Ebbe the Younger and her Companion-Martyrs
24	Bregwine, Archbishop of Canterbury

AUGUST (continued)

25	Ebbe the Elder, Abbess of Coldingham
26	Ninian, Bishop of Whithorn
	Pandwyna of Eltisley, Virgin
27	Decuman, Hermit and Martyr
29	Sebbe, King of the East Saxons, Monk
	Willeic, Abbot and Missionary *
	Edwold of Cerne, Hermit
30	Rumon, Irish missionary Bishop
31	Aidan, Bishop of Lindisfarne
	Cuthburgh and Cwenburgh, Abbesses of Wimborne
	Eanswyth, Abbess of Folkestone.

SEPTEMBER

01	Drithelm of Melrose, Monk
02	Heiu, Abbess of Tadcaster
03	Hereswith of Chelles Widow
	Balin, Monk
06	Felix and Augebert, Martyrs *
	Bega, Anchoress
07	Alcmund and Tilbert, Bishops of Hexham
08	Ethelburgh, Abbess of Lyminge
	Ina and Ethelburgh, King and Queen of Wessex
09	Bettelin of Crowland, Hermit
	Wulfhild, Abbess of Barking
10	Otger, Missionary
	Frithestan, Bishop of Winchester
13	Wilfrida, Abbess of Wilton
16	Edith of Wilton, Virgin
17	Socrates and Stephen, Martyrs in Britain *
19	Theodore of Tarsus, Archbishop of Canterbury
23	Cissa of Crowland, Hermit
25	Sigebert, King of East Anglia, Martyr
	Ceolfrith (Geoffrey), Abbot of Wearmouth
	Egelred of Crowland, Martyr
28	Tetta, Abbess of Wimborne

SEPTEMBER (continued)

28	Lioba, Abbess and Missionary
31	Eanswyth, Abbess of Folkestone
30	Honorius, Archbishop of Canterbury
	Tancred, Torthred and Tova, Hermits and Martyrs

OCTOBER

03	Ewald the Fair and Ewald the Dark, Martyrs
07	Osyth of Chich, Martyr
08	Iwi of Lindisfarne, Hermit
10	Paulinus, Archbishop of York
11	Ethelburgh, Abbess of Barking
12	Edwin, King and Martyr
	Wilfrid, Archbishop of York
14	Burchard, Bishop and Missionary *
15	Thecla of Wimborne, Abbess and Missionary
16	Vitalis, Hermit *
	Lull, Archbishop and Missionary
17	Ethelbert and Ailred, Martyrs
	Nothelm, Archbishop of Canterbury
19	Frideswide of Oxford, Virgin
	Ednoth, Bishop of Dorchester-on-Thames, Martyr
20	Acca, Bishop of Hexham
21	Tuda, Bishop of Northumbria
	Condedus, Hermit *
23	Elfleda of Glastonbury, Virgin
	Ethelfleda, Abbess of Romsey
26	Cedd, Apostle of Essex
	Edfrid, Abbot of Leominster, Confessor
	Eata, Bishop of Hexham
	Cuthbert, Archbishop of Canterbury
	Albinus, Bishop and Missionary *
28	Eadsige, Archbishop of Canterbury
30	Ethelnoth the Good, Archbishop of Canterbury
31	Begu, Nun
	Foillan, Missionary in East Anglia

NOVEMBER

03	Clodock, Hermit
	Wulgan, Confessor
	Rumwold of Northumbria, Confessor
04	Clair (Clarus), Priest and Martyr
	Birstan, Bishop of Winchester
05	Kea, Bishop in Devon
06	Edwen of Anglesey, Virgin *
07	Clement (Willibrord) of Northumbria, Apostle of the Frisians
08	Willehad, Bishop and Missionary
	Gregory, Abbot in Switzerland *
10	Justus, Archbishop of Canterbury
11	Berhtwine, Bishop *
12	Liafwine of Deventer, Missionary
	Ymar of Reculver, Martyr
14	Dubricius, missionary Bishop
16	Aelfric, Archbishop of Canterbury
17	Hilda, Abbess of Whitby
19	Ermenburgh, Abbess of Thanet
20	Edmund, King of East Anglia, Martyr
24	Enfleda, Abbess of Whitby
27	Congar, Abbot of Congresbury
29	Aylwine of Athelney, Monk

DECEMBER

03	Lucius, King in Britain *
	Birinus, Apostle of Wessex
	Sola, Hermit *
07	Diuma, Bishop and Missionary
08	Budoc, Celtic Missionary
	Gunthild of Wimborne, Virgin
09	Ethelgiva, Abbess of Shaftesbury
	Wolfeius, Hermit
12	Agatha of Wimborne, Virgin
13	Edburgh of Lyminge, Virgin
	Edburgh, Abbess of Minster-in-Thanet

DECEMBER (continued)

14	Hibald, Abbot
15	Offa, King of Essex, Monk
18	Winebald, Abbot and Missionary
23	Frithebert, Bishop of Hexham
25	Alburgh of Wilton, Nun
30	Egwin, Bishop of Worcester

DATE OF FEAST UNKNOWN

Blida, Holy Woman
Cett, Monk
Cuthfleda, Abbess of Leominster
Edburgh of Repton
Elphin, Patron of Warrington
Felgild of Farne, Hermit
Hwaetbert, Abbot of Wearmouth and Jarrow
Mindred, Holy Woman
Osanna, Holy Woman
Ostrythe, Queen of Mercia, Martyr
Ragener of Northampton, Martyr
Wendreda, Abbess of March
Weonard, Welsh Hermit
Withburgh of Ripon

Shire and Kingdom Index

BEDFORDSHIRE: Bedford, Dunstable

BERKSHIRE: Abingdon, Taplow

BUCKINGHAMSHIRE: Aylesbury, Buckingham, Wing

CAMBRIDGESHIRE: Chatteris, Eltisley, Ely, Eynesbury, March, Soham, Thorney

CHESHIRE: Chadkirk, Chester, Plemstall, Warburton, Winwick

CUMBERLAND: Briscoe, Caldew, Crossthwaite, Edenhall, Kirk Oswald, Mungrisedale, St. Bees, St. Herbert's Isle

DERBYSHIRE: Derby, Repton

DEVON: Braunton, Chittlehampton, Crediton, East Stowford, Exeter, Hartland, Landkey, Romansleigh, St. Budeaux, Tavistock

DORSET: Cerne, Cerne Abbas, Corfe, Horton, Langton Matravers, St. Aldhelm's Head, Shaftesbury, Sherborne, Wareham, Whitchurch Canonicorum, Wimborne

DURHAM: Chester-le-Street, Durham, Ebchester, Hartlepool, Jarrow, Monkton, Wearmouth

EAST ANGLIA

ESSEX: Barking, Bradwell-on-Sea, Colchester, Essex, London, Prittlewell, St. Osyth, Tilbury, Wakering, West Mersea

GLOUCESTERSHIRE: Aust, Aust Cliff, Coln St. Aldwyn, Deerhurst, Dyrham, Gloucester, Kingston-by-Thornbury, Lancant, Little Sodbury, St. Briavels, Tetbury, Westbury-on-Trym, Winchcombe

HAMPSHIRE: Bishops Waltham, Hampshire, Isle of Wight, Nursling, Romsey, Winchester

HEREFORDSHIRE: Archenfield, Clodock, Hereford, Kenderchurch, Leominster, Madley, Marden, St. Weonards, Sutton Walls.

HERTFORDSHIRE: St. Albans

HUNTINGDONSHIRE: Ramsey, St. Ives, St. Neots

KENT: Canterbury, Eastry, Folkestone, Hoo St. Werburgh, Kemsing, Lyminge, Minster-in-Sheppey, Minster-in-Thanet, Reculver, Rochester, Tenterden.

WILTSHIRE: Bishopstrow, Bradford-on-Avon, Malmesbury, Ramsbury, Wilton

WORCESTERSHIRE: Clent, Evesham, Pershore, Worcester

YORKSHIRE: Beverley, Catterick, Cotherstone, Coverdale, Crayke, Dewsbury, Easingwold, Everingham, Felixkirk, Gilling, Hackness, Harpham, Hatfield Chase, Hinderwell, Howden, Lastingham, Middleham, Oswaldkirk, Ripon, Romaldkirk, Tadcaster, Whitby, York.

General Bibliography

The Anglo-Saxon Chronicle, translated G. N. Garmonsway, Everyman, 1975.

Bede the Venerable. A History of the English Church and People, Penguin, 1974.

Bond, F.: *Dedications and Patron Saints of English Churches,* London 1914.

The Book of Saints, St. Augustine's Abbey, Ramsgate, Black 1921.

Butler, A.: *Lives of the Saints,* 4 vols., revised 1953–4.

Deanesly, M.: *The Pre-Conquest Church in England,* Black 1961.

Duckett, E. S.: *Saint Dunstan of Canterbury,* Collins 1955.

Ekwall, E.: *Dictionary of English Place-Names,* Oxford, 1987.

Farmer, D. H.: *The Oxford Dictionary of Saints,* 1978.

Godfrey, C. J.: *The Church in Anglo-Saxon England,* Cambridge 1962.

Hill, D.: *An Atlas of Anglo-Saxon England,* Blackwell 1981.

Kerr, M. & N.: *A Guide to Anglo-Saxon Sites,* 1982.

Lives of the Saints, translated J. F. Webb, Penguin, 1973.

Mayr-Harting, H.: *The Coming of Christianity to Anglo-Saxon England,* Batsford 1991.

Stenton, F.: *Anglo-Saxon England,* Oxford 1989.

Talbot, C. H.: *The Anglo-Saxon Missionaries in Germany,* Sheed and Ward 1981.

Taylor, H. M. & J.: *Anglo-Saxon Architecture,* 3 vols., Cambridge 1965–1978.

Sixty Saxon Saints
Alan Smith

Alan Smith has produced a useful concise guide which contains biographical details of most of the better known English saints and a calendar of their feast days.

The purpose of this booklet is to see some justice done to the English saints of the Anglo-Saxon period who took with them from the secular into the religious life the native English ideals of loyalty to one's Lord and, if necessary, sacrificial service to his cause.

This selection of saints includes some who were not of native birth but who are important to the story of English Christianity.

UK £2·95 net ISBN 1–898281–07–6 48pp

The Service of Prime from the Old English Benedictine Office
Text and Translation - Prepared by Bill Griffiths

The Old English Benedictine Office was a series of monastic daily services compiled in the late tenth or early eleventh centuries from the material that had largely already been translated from Latin into Old English. From that collection this version of the Old English Service of Prime was prepared for performance at the Anglo-Saxon church of St. Peter-on-the-Wall at Bradwell-on-Sea, Essex on 10th August 1991.

UK £2·50 net ISBN0–9516209–3–2 40pp

Looking for the Lost Gods of England
Kathleen Herbert

Kathleen Herbert sifts through the royal genealogies, charms, verse and other sources to find clues to the names and attributes of the Gods and Goddesses of the early English. The earliest account of English heathen practices reveals that they worshipped the Earth Mother and called her Nerthus. The tales, beliefs and traditions of that time are still with us and able to stir our minds and imaginations.

UK £4·95 net ISBN 1–898281–04–1 64pp

Anglo-Saxon Verse Charms, Maxims and Heroic Legends
Louis J. Rodrigues

The Germanic tribes who settled in Britain during the fifth and early sixth centuries brought with them a store of heroic and folk traditions: folk-tales, legends, rune-lore, magic charms against misfortune and illness, herbal cures, and the homely wisdom of experience enshrined in maxims and gnomic verse. Louis Rodrigues looks at the heroic and folk traditions that were recorded in verse, and which have managed to survive the depredations of time.

UK £7·95 net   ISBN 1–898281–01–7 176pp

Wordcraft
Concise English/Old English Dictionary and Thesaurus
Stephen Pollington

This book provides Old English equivalents to the commoner modern words in both dictionary and thesaurus formats. The Thesaurus presents vocabulary relevant to a wide range of individual topics in alphabetical lists, thus making it easily accessible to those with specific areas of interest. Each thematic listing is encoded for cross-reference from the Dictionary. The two sections will be of invaluable assistance to students of the language, as well as to those with either a general or a specific interest in the Anglo-Saxon period.

UK £9·95 net ISBN 1–898281–02–5 256pp

Spellcraft
Old English Heroic Legends
Kathleen Herbert

The author has taken the skeletons of ancient Germanic legends about great kings, queens and heroes, and put flesh on them. Kathleen Herbert's extensive knowledge of the period is reflected in the wealth of detail she brings to these tales of adventure, passion, bloodshed and magic.

The book is in two parts. First are the stories that originate deep in the past, yet because they have not been hackneyed, they are still strange and enchanting. After that there is a selection of the source material, with information about where it can be found and some discussion about how it can be used.

UK £6·95 net ISBN 0–9516209–9–1 288pp

Monasteriales Indicia
The Anglo-Saxon Monastic Sign Language
Edited with notes and translation by
Debby Banham

The *Monasteriales Indicia* is one of very few texts which let us see how life was really lived in monasteries in the early Middle Ages. Written in Old English and preserved in a manuscript of the mid-eleventh century, it consists of 127 signs used by Anglo-Saxon monks during the times when the Benedictine Rule forbade them to speak. These indicate the foods the monks ate, the clothes they wore, and the books they used in church and chapter, as well as the tools they used in their daily life, and persons they might meet both in the monastery and outside. The text is printed here with a parallel translation.

UK £6·95 net ISBN 0–9516209–4–0 96pp

Handbook of Anglo-Saxon Food:
Processing and Consumption
Ann Hagen

For the first time information from various sources has been brought together in order to build up a picture of how food was grown, conserved, prepared and eaten during the period from the beginning of the 5th century to the 11th century. No specialist knowledge of the Anglo-Saxon period or language is needed, and many people will find it fascinating for the views it gives of an important aspect of Anglo-Saxon life and culture. In addition to Anglo-Saxon England the Celtic west of Britain is also covered.

UK £7·95 net ISBN 0–9516209–8–3 192pp

An Introduction to
the Old English Language and its Literature
Stephen Pollington

The purpose of this general introduction to Old English is not to deal with the teaching of Old English but to dispel some misconceptions about the language and to give an outline of its structure and its literature. Some basic knowledge of these is essential to an understanding of the early period of English history and the present form of the language.

UK £2·95 net ISBN 1–898281–06–8 28pp

Anglo-Saxon Runes
John. M. Kemble

Kemble's essay *On Anglo-Saxon Runes* first appeared in the journal *Archaeologia* for 1840; it draws on the work of Wilhelm Grimm, but breaks new ground for Anglo-Saxon studies in his survey of the Ruthwell Cross and the Cynewulf poems. For this edition, new notes have been supplied, which include translations of Latin and Old English material quoted in the text, to make this key work in the study of runes more accessible to the general reader.

UK £6·95 net ISBN 0–9516209–1–6 80pp

The Battle of Maldon: Text and Translation
Translated and edited by Bill Griffiths

The Battle of Maldon was fought between the men of Essex and the Vikings in AD 991. The action was captured in an Anglo-Saxon poem whose vividness and heroic spirit has fascinated readers and scholars for generations. *The Battle of Maldon* includes the source text; edited text; parallel literal translation; verse translation; review of 103 books and articles.

UK £4·95 net ISBN 0–9516209–0–8 96pp

Alfred's Metres of Boethius
Edited by Bill Griffiths

In this new edition of the Old English *Metres of Boethius*, clarity of text, informative notes and a helpful glossary have been a priority, for this is one of the most approachable of Old English verse texts, lucid and delightful; its relative neglect by specialists will mean this text will come as a new experience to many practised students of the language; while its clear, expositional verse style makes it an ideal starting point for all amateurs of the period.

UK £14·95 net   ISBN 1–898281–03–3   B5   212pp

Beowulf: Text and Translation
Translated by John Porter

The verse in which the story unfolds is, by common consent, the finest writing surviving in Old English, a text that all students of the language and many general readers will want to tackle in the original form. To aid understanding of the Old English, a literal word-by-word translation by John Porter is printed opposite an edited text and provides a practical key to this Anglo-Saxon masterpiece.

UK £7·95 net   ISBN 0–9516209–2–4   192pp

The Homecoming of Beorhtnoth
J. R. R. Tolkien

The Homecoming of Beorhtnoth contains a short play about two men who were sent by the monks of Ely to recover the body of Beorhtnoth from the battlefield. There is also a piece about the Old English poem *The Battle of Maldon* and criticism of Beorhtnoth's tactics. A special limited edition of 300 numbered copies has been printed, with the permission of the Tolkien Estate, to commemorate the 1000th anniversary of the Battle of Maldon.

Only available direct from Anglo-Saxon Books at £3·50   28pp

For orders totalling less than £5 please add 50 pence for post and packing.
For a full list of publications including our new series of booklets send a s.a.e. to:

Anglo-Saxon Books
25 Malpas Drive, Pinner, Middlesex. HA5 1DQ England
Tel: 081-868 1564

Most titles are available in North America from:
Paul & Company Publishers Consortium Inc.
c/o PCS Data Processing Inc., 360 West 31 St., New York, NY 10001
Tel: (212) 564-3730 ext. 264

Þa Engliscan Gesiðas

Þa Engliscan Gesiðas (The English Companions) is a historical and cultural society exclusively devoted to Anglo-Saxon history. Its aims are to bridge the gap between scholars and non-experts, and to bring together all those with an interest in the Anglo-Saxon period, its language, culture and traditions, so as to promote a wider interest in, and knowledge of all things Anglo-Saxon. The Fellowship publishes a journal, *Wiðowinde*, which helps members to keep in touch with current thinking on topics from art and archaeology to heathenism and Early English Christianity. The Fellowship enables like-minded people to keep in contact by publicising conferences, courses and meetings that might be of interest to its members. A correspondence course in Old English is also available.

For further details write to:
The Membership Secretary, Þa Engliscan Gesiðas
BM Box 4336, London, WC1N 3XX England.

Regia Anglorum

Regia Anglorum is a society that was founded to accurately re-create the life of the British people as it was around the time of the Norman Conquest. Our work has a strong educational slant and we consider authenticity to be of prime importance. We prefer, where possible, to work from archaeological materials and are extremely cautious regarding such things as the interpretation of styles depicted in manuscripts. Approximately twenty-five per cent of our membership, of over 500 people, are archaeologists or historians.

The Society has a large working Living History Exhibit, teaching and exhibiting more than twenty crafts in an authentic environment. We own a forty foot wooden ship replica of a type that would have been a common sight in Northern European waters around the turn of the first millennium AD. Battle re-enactment is another aspect of our activities, often involving 200 or more warriors.

For further information contact:
K. J. Siddorn, 9 Durleigh Close, Headley Park,
Bristol BS13 7NQ, England.

West Stow Anglo-Saxon Village

An early Anglo-Saxon Settlement reconstructed on the site where it was excavated consisting of timber and thatch hall, houses and workshop. Open all year 10a.m. – 4.15p.m. (except Yule). Free taped guides. Special provision for school parties. A teachers' resource pack is available. Costumed events are held at weekends, especially Easter Sunday and August Bank Holiday Monday. Craft courses are organised.

Details available from:
The Visitor Centre, West Stow Country Park
Icklingham Road, West Stow
Bury St Edmunds, Suffolk IP28 6HG
Tel: 0284 728718